What Do You Mean the Third Dimension is Going Away?

Why now is the time to release who you are not and remember who you are

Enjoy the Journey
Jim

INNER SIGHT PRESS

What Do You Mean the Third Dimension is Going Away?

Why now is the time to release who you are not and remember who you are

**Jim Self
Roxane Burnett**

INNER SIGHT PRESS

© Jim Self, Roxane Burnett 2013

All rights reserved. No part of this book may be reproduced by any mechanical, photographic, or electronic process, or in the form of a phonographic recording; nor may it be stored in a retrieval system, transmitted, or otherwise be copied for public or private use—other than for "fair use" as brief quotations embodied in articles and reviews without prior written of the publisher.

The authors of this book do not dispense medical advice or prescribe the use of any technique as a form of treatment for physical or medical problems without the advice of a physician, either directly or indirectly. The intent of the authors is only to offer information to help you in your quest for emotional and spiritual well-being. In the event you use any of the information in this book for yourself, which is your constitutional right, the authors and the publisher assume no responsibility for your actions.

ISBN 978-0-9885760-0-1

Edited by Sandra Sedgbeer
Cover and interior design by Damian Keenan,
Cover concept by Roxane Burnett and Jim Self
Audio Editing by Peggy Ann Kerr
Printed and bound in the USA

1 2 3 4 5 6 7 8 9 17 16 15 14 13

Published by Inner Sight Press

7021 E. Earll Dr. # 103,
Scottsdale, AZ 85251

CONTENTS

Jim's Introduction 13
Roxane's Introduction 19

SECTION I
WHAT IS HAPPENING TO MY WORLD? 23

1 The 'Shift' – What is it?
  And How is it Affecting You? 24
  Remembering who you are ♦ The Waves of Change—
  How and why this is happening now ♦ How the Shift might
  be affecting you ♦ Ascension symptoms? ♦ Whose thoughts
  are these anyway? ♦ Time is going faster ♦ Losing your
  memories, remembering your Self

2 Mastering Alchemy And Creating Your Own
  Heaven on Earth 36
  What is Mastering Alchemy? ♦ How can you learn to
  master it? ♦ Where will it take you?

3 Understanding the Game of the Third Dimension
  And How to Play It 40
  The third dimensional box ♦ Understanding our third
  dimensional experience ♦ The third dimensional matrix
  and structures ♦ Duality ♦ Reactionary present time ♦ The
  rational mind

CONTENTS

4 The Fourth Dimensional Matrix and Structures 53
Present time ♦ Choice ♦ Paradox ♦ Alignment and balance ♦ What is the fifth dimension?

5 Mastering Fourth Dimensional Present Time 63
Allowing the Shift to clear your unconscious thoughts and feelings ♦ Understanding the lower and higher fourth dimension

6 The Seven Layers of Thought 72
Shoot, ready, aim ♦ Arguing in your head ♦ Curious without being engaged ♦ Conscious, focused, capable ♦ Accessing deeper awareness ♦ Where the thought that thought you into existence and you think together

7 A Simple Truth About the Law of Attraction 80
Your attention on your intention—using the Law of Attraction ♦ Reverse engineering the Law of Attraction ♦ Experience the power of your thought

8 Alchemy: Changing the Frequency of Thought, Altering the Harmonics of Matter, and Applying the Element of Love 89
Thoughts are electrical, emotions are magnetic ♦ Thoughts don't just disappear ♦ Changing how you feel changes everything ♦ Applying the element of Love ♦ Creating your desired result

CONTENTS

SECTION II
TOOLS TO REBUILD YOURSELF 97

9 The Path and Purpose of These Tools 98
Getting the most out of this work ♦ Being in reaction ♦ Quitting before you begin, or getting tangled in the rational mind ♦ Believing that you are not clairvoyant ♦ Staying attached to old patterns of relationships

10 **Tool # 1 – Reclaiming Your Command Center, Finding the Center of Your Head** 107
Returning the energy of others back to them ♦ What you may notice

11 **Tool # 2 – The Gift of Grounding—Whose Thoughts Are These Anyway?** 114
Two elements to the Grounding Cord ♦ Releasing the thoughts and emotions that don't belong to you

12 **Tool # 3 – The Rose** 120
Why a Rose and not a turnip? ♦ A bit about the aura ♦ Establishing, defining and holding your space ♦ How not to feel the pain of others ♦ Making separations from others ♦ Releasing limiting beliefs and habits

13 **Tool # 4 – Your Higher Mind** 141
Finding your Higher Mind

14 **Tool # 5 – The Octahedron—The Diamond of Light Surrounding You** 144
Constructing the Octahedron

CONTENTS

15 Tool # 6 – Activating Your Personal Power Field 150
  Spinning the Octahedron and More: A story from Jim

16 Tool # 7 – The Living Words 160
  Words as vibrations ♦ Choosing Happy

17 Using The Tools to Make Your Job More Fun 169
  How to make meetings successful for *you*

18 Tool # 8 – The Strength of Silence 175
  The advantages of quietness ♦ Mastering the art of quiet observation

19 Where Do All These Tools Lead? 179
  What we have observed in ourselves and in others ♦ What is now available to you ♦ The Sanctuary of the Pink Diamond ♦ The Three Kingdoms ♦ Journeys to the temples ♦ Other Geometries ♦ Flying ♦ The Rays of Creation

SECTION III
ADVANCING YOUR SKILLS 183

20 You Are Rewiring Yourself 184
  Moving from being unconscious to being aware ♦ What can make the rewiring happen faster?

21 You Are Not Your Problem 187
  Developing the skill of discernment

CONTENTS

22 Developing Your Clairvoyance 192
You already are intuitive

23 Relationships—The Biggest Game on The Planet 196
A truth about masculine and feminine energy ♦ The 4 typical types of masculine and feminine interaction ♦ How did we get so out of whack? ♦ Bringing your masculine and feminine energy into alignment ♦ Becoming aware in your daily life of how you create

24 How to Create a Hot, Healthy, Higher Relationship 221
Being self-ish ♦ Me Bubbles and We Bubbles ♦ I love me when I'm with you

25 Sympathy, Empathy and Compassion 232
The chakras as barometers of balance or imbalance ♦ Reaction versus response

26 More on The Power of Words to Rewire 237
A triangular platform upon which to stand ♦ Your colors change ♦ The words and their vibrations begin to be anchored in your energy field ♦ You begin to activate aspects of your Light Body

27 The Benefits of Mastering Your Attention Point 244
Observing without labeling ♦ Using the conscious, continuous breath as a tool for focusing your attention point ♦ What you will notice as you become more masterful

CONTENTS

28 Tricking Your Brain Into Awareness 249
Two states of awareness ♦ Changing the routine ♦ Creating a new pathway

29 Understanding the Difference Between Your Higher Self and Your Soul 255

30 The Higher Purpose of Your Ego 258

31 Your New Life In the Fifth Dimension 261
The door to the fifth dimension ♦ Time in the fifth dimension ♦ Standing on the platform of the higher dimensions ♦ The long-awaited 'Shift of the Ages' is upon us ♦ Unveiling the experiment ♦ Revealing the true nature of the experiment

Success Stories 273

Epilogue: How Do We Know All This? 285

About the Authors
Jim Self 287
Roxane Burnett 289

What is Mastering Alchemy? 291

Jim's Introduction

What do we mean when we say "the third dimension is going away"? There is a shift in consciousness occurring. It is a shift in the perception of our world. Many feel that something is not right, that something has been lost. In our rush to create more for ourselves, the bigger house, a better car, a higher salary, we have actually created less. We have less time to spend in that big house, less time to enjoy the company of our family and friends and less opportunity to appreciate a sunset or take pleasure in the natural beauty that surrounds us. What is really missing, whether we're aware of it or not, is that we have lost a part of our 'selves' along the way. And at the end of the day, more, bigger and better are simply not enough. We have disconnected from the things that truly nourish us, and it has left us physically ill, emotionally unhappy, mentally exhausted and spiritually unclear about who we truly are.

This, however, is beginning to change.

As more and more of us begin to shift, we are starting to remember who we are. We are recognizing imbalances in our lives and asking ourselves *What's really important to me? What truly makes me happy?* The answer isn't found by gaining more of the world outside but in gaining more of the 'me' within. In our rush to the top, we have left a part of ourselves behind. We have traded respect for competition, kindness for advantage and giving for taking. We've lost touch with our 'inner guidance', which always directs us to a higher, more vibrant place. This higher place is a place where cooperation, support and understanding create deeper trust, friendship and compassion.

A shift is occurring within the hearts of humanity now, and millions are beginning consciously to awaken. They are finding a new passion within and recognizing that who they are counts. "I AM valuable, important and significant. I matter, and I have a contribution to make!" This passion is being reignited within each of us. This shift is taking place across the world in every town and village and in the hearts of each man, woman and child. Whether the issue is feeding the poor, healing the sick, building community, or nurturing the Earth, there is a growing awareness. It is an awakening—a Shift in Consciousness! A connection is being made one heart to another. In this connection of caring, sharing, giving and receiving, a spark within the heart has been ignited and is growing. This awakening consciousness has no limits. It is a shift that is taking us all into a higher dimensional awareness; a higher, more aligned way of life. We are 'becoming aware of becoming aware'.

This is what we mean when we say that the third dimension is going away. In simple terms, it is the old habits of thinking, feeling, and behaving that we know as the third dimension that are going away. As this Shift in consciousness is demonstrating, everyone is shifting into a fourth dimensional consciousness and experience, and then into a fifth dimensional consciousness and experience.

However, many people on the planet are not prepared for this Shift. And for those who are unaware of what is going on, this transition will not be an easy or comfortable experience because we cannot take our mental and emotional baggage with us.

But this transition can be a wonderful, enjoyable time, as well. With some basic information about what the Shift is, and what 'dimensions' are, and with some simple tools to help manage our thoughts and feelings, *everyone* has the ability to evolve their consciousness, release their mental and emotional baggage, and move gracefully and joyfully into these higher vibrational realms.

If you don't know what dimensions are, you are not alone. Most people playing the game of life as we know it in the third dimension are playing without a 'rule book' to explain what the game really is and how one can play it successfully.

This book provides these basic, missing rules. It explains more thoroughly what the Shift is all about, why it's happening now, and how it's affecting all of us. It also explains what the third dimension, fourth, and fifth dimensions are, and why they are the most important consideration of your life right now. Because if you can understand the structure and play of these dimensions, you can begin to move fluidly through the unprecedented changes of this Shift without fear, without effort, without the tension and anxiety that is, for the most part, the daily habit of our lives.

Most importantly, it provides you with some simple yet profound energy tools that can help you to step out of the noise and drama of the third dimension and manage your thoughts in every moment. These tools, as part of our Mastering Alchemy Program, have helped thousands of people around the world. And now we're sharing them with you, so that you too can be prepared for the unprecedented opportunity and challenge of living and creating in *present time* in the higher dimensions.

You see we already have the potential, all the necessary equipment and wiring, right now, to be fully conscious in all these dimensions. But our habits of thinking and feeling, grooved over many lifetimes, dumb us down and limit us to a third dimensional experience. Our left-brain, rational mind only knows what it knows and doesn't know what it doesn't know, and it works tirelessly to keep us within a thin range of objective third dimensional thinking and possibilities. And we, for the most part, have gone along for the ride.

But no longer.

The increasing light energies and frequencies of the Shift are rewiring our brains to allow us access to a much wider range of information and possibilities than are available in the third dimension. These light energies are preparing us for the fourth and fifth dimensional experiences, even as they are clearing the rigidity of the third dimensional 'rules' from our consciousness.

The vast majority of people on this planet are not prepared to be the masters of their every thought, feeling, and action in every moment. But there's no option. It's a required, baseline skill of higher fourth dimensional and fifth dimensional consciousness.

As third dimensional linear time is collapsing into a single point of *present time*, the time buffer between our thoughts and our creations is collapsing too. We have less opportunity to practice being aware of our mental and emotional habits before *what we think is what we get*. This is a very big deal.

If you practice using the tools offered in this book now, when it doesn't absolutely count, they will become your habit when it does count. And you will begin to realign gracefully with the fullness of *You*.

Easy? Kind of… Simple? Yes.

Does it require awareness and a choice from a present time space? Absolutely.

Can you sit on the sidelines and hope it all turns out? No.

Increased levels of electromagnetic light from the higher dimensions are now flowing within all of us. Many people in the third dimension cannot handle this surge, and they are choosing to step out of their bodies.

And many, many more will follow as the Shift accelerates. You see, *everyone* is going home to the fourth and then fifth dimensions, but not everyone is going home on the same timeline, and with the same ease and grace.

How do you choose?

As the shift accelerates and time collapses and *everything* is in the present moment, you could still choose your thoughts and feelings unconsciously, out of third dimensional habit, and you would have the opportunity to live that discomfort fully and immediately in your experience. Or you can choose your thought and emotion in every moment, with focus and awareness, and live the fullness of that experience.

In other words, it's to your benefit to practice and integrate the ability to choose the contents of your consciousness right now before it really counts—and that moment is not very far away.

It's all up to you.

The third dimension is going away. But we are at the beginning of this new way of life, not the end. Each of us must awaken now. Each must make the shift within. Until now, the center of your head, the place from where you can choose your thoughts and attention point, has been pre-occupied by the thoughts of others. Your Mom-Dad-Teacher-Minister loved you and had an opinion about the best way for you to live your life, and as their thoughts moved into your head, 'You' moved out.

Now it is time to take back ownership of the center of your head. It's time to start living in alignment with the heart, and experience the vibrations and consequences of concepts such as *I like me, I'm happy, I'm pleased with myself.*

It's time to release who you are not and discover who you *really* are.

Roxane's Introduction

So what would you think if you and your life partner were happily going about your business of teaching simple, practical energy tools for years in a small town and one day something comes out of his mouth that stuns you? I'd been content with small classes, successfully teaching and mentoring others and making big changes in my own life for almost a decade when, out of the blue, Jim says: "None of what we have been doing has been random. We thought it was at the time. In fact, I thought I was just making all this up. But it wasn't random. There is an underlying purpose to it all."

Wouldn't that make you stop and wonder? Purpose? What purpose? I thought we were doing this because our students were having huge insights and major life changes. We were simply having fun and enjoying creating with each other. I was content.

After Jim said that (and I had picked myself off the floor), I began to think back over the years and consider the tools we presented, many of which you now hold in this book. I was able to trace the progression of the continually new and expanding tools from the beginning (1994) to where we are now, and I could indeed see an evolution. And possibly a purpose!

He was right. Nothing we had ever presented was random, and it still isn't, even if we don't know exactly where it is all leading. We do have some clues, however. The Shift of Consciousness is upon us, and it is affecting all of humanity. According to the thousands who have used them, these tools are the best things to ease the transition. They remove the old programing and give you new, solid reference points to recreate your life.

Another clue is that many millions are awakening from a deep sleep and asking big questions. They thirst for something solid to hang onto that will work—*really work*—for them. Clue number three is that this work has moved from being just 21 people in a small town in California to thousands all over the globe. The work and play is now a living, breathing, expanding consciousness, moving across the planet with very little effort from us. We are humbled and thrilled that so many can use these tools and be who they came here to be. Contentment has turned into passion. And purpose.

Some notes about how this book is presented:

1. It is sometimes tricky when two people write a book together. We thought it would be easier for you to read if we used the word "we." Occasionally there will be a reference to "I." It will be clear who is speaking then.

2. At the end of many of the chapters there is a QR Code and a URL to a private page that is not accessible through the front door of our website. These pages contain additional MP3 audio files and videos featuring meditations, exercises, and expanded information to enhance your experience of, and ability to, master the tools.

3. You will read many familiar words that have new meanings or describe unique concepts. We have italicized these—i.e., *present time, going to, paradox,* etc.

4. The names of the tools themselves will be capitalized—Rose, Living Words, Higher Mind, etc.

5. Words used as the Living Words, will also be capitalized—Certain, Gracious, Capable, etc.

I know you'll get the hang of it very quickly. It is a new language in many ways. The key is to put your rational mind on vacation and don't try to figure this out. There is much energy loaded into these written words, MP3s and videos. Your rational mind will only get in the way and confuse you.

This work and play, information and tools, may not be for you.

In fact, they are for the very few among us. This is because only those most committed to their path, their personal evolution and growth, are intentional enough to experiment with them. The tools are extremely simple and easy to use, but they change lives in big ways and some people are just not ready for change, even though they may say they are.

There are many options available today for self-growth; many workshops, DVDs, webinars, teachers and leaders. Most are very entertaining. Many people take the weekend seminar, feel good for a few days, and then can't remember how to get back to that good feeling place. What we share with you is entertaining and fun, but it isn't for your entertainment. It is not designed for the mass third dimensional collective, but only for those who truly want to focus their attention, practice the tools and get somewhere. And if you are one of those, hang on to your seat. Because you WILL indeed get 'somewhere'—somewhere really indescribably grand.

Home.

... With all the love there is,

Roxane

SECTION I

What Is Happening to My World?

CHAPTER ONE

The 'Shift' – What is it?
And How is it Affecting You?

There is a change underway, a Shift that is affecting every aspect of our third dimensional (3D) reality. This Shift is so far-reaching that our limited imagination cannot begin to grasp the magnitude of the changes we are now experiencing. As part of this transition, almost everything we have taken for granted is falling away. The rigid frameworks that once dictated the way nations, cultures, and individuals experience themselves in our third dimensional societies are unraveling.

The Shift is not only altering our consciousness, it is changing the world around us. A shift, by definition, is the 'movement from one position to another' or a 'change in direction', This Shift is affecting every aspect of life on the planet; our political, social and economic structures, the environment, the weather, every institution, all the wars, how we view our relationships, our work, every thought we think, and every feeling we feel. It is altering time, our memory, our DNA, the wiring of our physical and emotional bodies, our beliefs, our perceptions of good and bad, right and wrong, and, most especially, our awareness of what is possible.

When we look a little deeper, however, we also find that there is a new passion growing. Individuals, groups, communities and companies are offering new ideas to clean the Earth, recycle waste, and create new power sources. More companies offer employee ownership, day care, alternative health care, equal pay and much more. More small businesses are being created and many are thriving.

The Shift is providing new understandings of how to once again live in harmony with each other, the Earth and All That Is, and the evidence is everywhere. Together we are becoming a unified consciousness within a global community. The duality of opposites: black and white, East and West, right and wrong, us and them, good and bad, and male and female is changing. The dividing lines are becoming less distinct. We are moving from the third dimensional experience of separation and extremes to a way of life that allows for many greater possibilities, connected communities, and expanding ease and well-being.

However, between this new 'Heaven on Earth' and where we currently exist there is transition.

Remembering *who you are*

The Shift we are experiencing is a shift in our very perception of the world. As most of us have played this game of life, we have tried to fit in and follow the rules. We have tried to create a better life for ourselves—the bigger house, better car, higher salary, etc. In the process, many have discovered that we have actually created *less*. We have less time to spend in that big house, less time to enjoy the company of our family and friends, and less opportunity to appreciate a sunset or take pleasure in the natural beauty that surrounds us. Many people have begun to feel that something is not right, that something valuable has been lost. What is really missing, whether we are aware of it or not, is that we all have lost a part of our 'selves' along the way. And at the end of the day, *more, bigger and better* has become less, smaller and stressful. We have disconnected from the things that truly nourish us and it has left us physically ill, emotionally unhappy, mentally exhausted, and spiritually unclear about *who we truly are*.

This is now beginning to change.

As more and more of us are awakening, we are beginning to remember who we are. We are recognizing imbalances in our lives and we are asking ourselves: 'What's really important to me? What truly makes me happy?' The answer isn't found through gaining more of the world *outside*, but in gaining more of the 'me' *within*.

In our rush to the top we left a part of ourselves behind. We traded respect for competition, kindness for advantage, and giving for taking. We lost touch with our 'inner guidance', which has always directed us to a higher, more aligned place, where cooperation, support and understanding create deeper trust, alignment and balance.

The Shift is occurring within the hearts of ALL of humanity and millions are beginning to awaken. It is an 'awakening of consciousness!' It is taking place across the world in every town and village and in the hearts of each child, woman and man. We are finding a new passion within, and we are beginning to recognize that *who* we are counts. We ALL matter, and we ALL have *a contribution to make*. Whether the issue is feeding the poor, healing the sick, building community, or nurturing the Earth, there is a growing awareness. It is an awakening—a Shift in Consciousness. A connection is being made one heart to another. In this connection of caring, sharing, giving and receiving, a spark within the heart ignites and grows. This awakening consciousness has no limits. It is a shift that is taking us all into a higher dimensional awareness; a higher, more aligned way of life. We are 'becoming aware of becoming aware'.

The Shift is occurring. It is a grand movement toward a life of integrity, grace and well-being. The transition between where we are and where we are going may be bumpy and challenging, but it is also very exciting. Regardless of whether we embrace the changes or resist them, we are moving forward to a way of life and a way of being that is closer to *who we truly are*.

The Waves of Change – How this is happening

The Shift is being driven by two huge Waves of Light that hold massive amounts of information and instructions. Over the past few years these waves have been rewiring our DNA, upgrading our bodies' physical, emotional and mental systems, and activating the fourth and fifth dimensional (4D and 5D) chakras, aligning us with a higher awareness.

One Wave is expanding outward, like an ever-widening ripple on a pond, spreading greater Light, knowledge and wisdom, opening ever-expanding gateways to higher consciousness and evolution. It is shifting mass consciousness from the third dimensional perspective, through the fourth, into a fifth dimensional perspective. This Wave is creating a fifth dimensional community of higher consciousness on Earth that is realigning us with the All That Is.

In addition to this new Wave of expanding consciousness there's another, equally powerful Wave. Its function is to create harmony. However, in order to achieve harmony, everything that is not of the Light, everything that does not exist in well-being and balance is being destabilized, dissolved and cleared away. In short, everything that is no longer working in our lives is being loosened and released.

This Wave is releasing all dysfunctional patterns on every level. All that is lacking in integrity will dissolve and be replaced with new aligned patterns of energy. In short, as one Wave of Light is emptying the vessel, the other Wave of Light is simultaneously refilling it. These Waves work in tandem to clear from each of us *who we are not*. All the old thoughts, habits, and emotions that whisper loudly to each of us are moving out as we remember *who we are*. These two transformative Waves are allowing all of us to rewire, reconnect, realign and remember who we really are and what we came here to accomplish. Like a tsunami, these Waves are significantly stepping up in intensity. We will see tremendous transitions over the months and years ahead.

Why is this all happening now?

This is all happening now because *we* have asked for it to occur. It is also happening now because we have been very successful. In the most amazing way, we have accomplished what we came here to achieve by playing this game of the third dimension. And it is now time to remember, and to return Home to the Heart of the Creator, the All That Is.

You see, everyone is going Home to the higher dimensions, but not everyone is going Home on the same timeline, and with the same ease and grace.

As long ago as the 16th century, William Shakespeare wrote "All the world's a stage, and all the men and women merely players." Shakespeare wasn't just a great playwright; he was a very wise man, for life on this planet is indeed a Grand Play. And now we are coming to the end of Act 3—the Final Act. This is where we get to bring our Grand Play to its finale and go Home. Not as in dying or leaving the body, but more like the caterpillar becoming the butterfly.

Going Home is precisely what the Shift is all about. The Shift is clearing away all that we are not, and assisting us in rewiring the connections, so that we can finally remember all that we are.

However, this is not going to happen without some attention on our part. To complete this experiment we signed up for, we now have the opportunity to put our 'selves' back together again. This is where the mastering of Alchemy, the rearranging of yourself, comes into play. Learning to put yourself back together, and to rebuild your Personal Power Field, using some very specific tools is what this book is all about. This is your journey Home and it is very possible.

So, is this something to be happy about? Yes!

Could you be excited? Yes!

Is it simple? Yes!

Is it going to be easy? Not exactly… but it does not have to be difficult either.

How the Shift might be affecting you

A deep, personal, internal Shift is stirring as the long-promised awakening is manifesting. Many people around the world are now awakening and remembering who they are and why they came here. Others are suddenly finding themselves experiencing feelings, situations, and emotions for which they have no frame of reference.

The transformation that is occurring within us is shifting our thoughts, making us question our beliefs, and changing the ways in which we experience the world around us. Until now, most have measured themselves by the outside world. Our beliefs about how we look, what is acceptable, what we think, and how we act have all been established by the third dimensional world outside of ourselves.

As exciting and as wonderful as this transition is, it is also creating difficulties for many. These difficulties are occurring as the pace quickens and we continue to hold tightly to our third dimensional beliefs and habits, and how we judge others for their actions, or try to fix them because 'we know better'. These choices belong to the third dimension and they must be released. As long as we continue to hold these limitations, and argue for the 'rights' and 'wrongs', we will experience the effects of the Shift within our physical and emotional bodies. These effects are known as Ascension Symptoms.

What are Ascension Symptoms?

Many people have been experiencing odd symptoms such as dizziness, confusion, headaches, loss of focus, fatigue, digestive discomfort, anxiety, or cold or warm spots on areas of the body, etc.

You also may be experiencing this as a loss of time in your day. Is there more on your plate and less time in which to complete it? You may be losing aspects of your memories. Things—and even people—that once seemed very important to you may be becoming less important. You may be spending more time alone, and enjoying it. Many people are also feeling a heightened sense of distraction, coupled with an emotional sense that something is 'just not right'. You may be among them. If so, there are two things that are useful to know: you are not alone, and there is no need to be alarmed.

What's going on here is that as we argue for our limitations and hold on to the old beliefs that no longer support us, we are creating a resistance or blockage within our four-body system that is causing discomfort. As we said earlier, the third dimensional reality as we have known it is shifting. Your awareness is becoming grander, and it is becoming far more aligned and balanced as you move into a higher consciousness. Humanity is waking up, and as it does, the old structures that have supported duality, maintained separation, and controlled the masses with fear are beginning to crumble.

Whose thoughts are these anyway?

Our thoughts create our beliefs, our beliefs create our habits, and our habits create our lives. In other words, our thoughts, no matter how unconscious, create our reality. However, many of the thoughts that we think and the beliefs that we hold are not even our own. They were given to us by our mom, dad, teacher, minister and the third dimensional reality outside of us. It's not that Mom and Dad, or anyone else around us, set out deliberately to mislead us. In most cases it was because they loved and wanted the best for us. Their guidance was very specific: "Do this, don't do that. This is good and right, that's bad and wrong. Talk to these people and not to those people…" You get the picture. These caring adults were simply passing on to us what *their* parents and their parent's parents (along with most of the rest of society) had taught them to accept as the 'truth'.

Growing up, many of us may intuitively have felt that what others accepted as the 'truth' did not feel 'right' or congruent to us, but consensus opinion is a powerful thing. It's not easy to stand up against the crowd or argue with our elders or loved ones. Hence, many of us learned to 'fit in'—to repress our intuitive senses, and dumb down our feelings. In the process, we became numb. This is why so many people today are unhappy but have no idea why. It's because they have lost touch with their own inner guidance system; that internal spark that wants to scream, "YES, this is who I AM!"

As we each begin to awaken, seek our own truth, and walk our own unique path, we begin to realize that there is much more to *who we are* than the outside world would lead us to believe. As we look within, we begin to realize that we are bigger, multi-dimensional spiritual beings able to align with a Higher Truth. As this transformation occurs, a new recognition unfolds: *it is our own truth that creates happiness and adds simplicity to our path.*

In the past, few have experienced this Higher Truth. But now this truth is an expanding presence sought by many. Because of you and the many others who are now awakening, a new consciousness is unfolding! The third dimensional world that was once defined by the old truths, structures and beliefs of those around us is no longer working for those that are now awakening. That third dimensional game is being dissolved. Moreover, linear time as we have known it—past, present and future—is also changing as we awaken to our Higher Truths.

Time is going faster

Time is more related to the rhythms and cycles held within our four bodies than it is to the clock on the wall. As these two massive Waves of Light flow within, through, and around Earth and us, all the reference points that we have come to know ourselves by are also changing.

The first change that is occurring is in the Earth's magnetic fields. The Waves of Light are altering the magnetic fields that surround Earth, causing them to weaken, deteriorate and change. As the planet's magnetic fields change, the cycles, rhythms and magnetic fields within our spiritual, mental, emotional and physical bodies are also being altered. Some cycles are accelerating while others are slowing down. And as the Waves of Light pass through each of us, our concept of time is being altered. Although the internal sensation is that time is speeding up, we are, in reality, losing time. Time is not going faster, but rather, is collapsing. The past and future are disappearing. We are now becoming aware of a much more simple form of time—*present time*. Time is condensing into a single moment of *present time now*.

In *present time* we can make *new* choices. In *present time*, negative emotional reactions from past experiences will no longer influence our choices. *Choice* in the *now moment* is neither based on past beliefs nor on future fears.

Losing your memories, remembering your Self

To further enhance our *present time* experiences, making this Shift even more interesting, we are also losing our memories. And no, it is not Alzheimer's. Neither does it have anything to do with your gender, age or culture. As you know, the purpose of one Wave of Light is to clear away old patterns, beliefs, thoughts and emotions that we hold that do not support our well-being—the *who we are not*. Because we did not know what to do with the insults or invalidations we received growing up, we learned to hide them away. In so doing, we chose to give up our own seniority and individual identity, and instead we accepted the opinions of others. Now, as we begin to awaken and remember who we truly are, many of our old untrue, non-aligned belief patterns are beginning to rise to the surface and fall away. In this process we are losing many of our old memories, and the reference points upon which we have built our third dimensional reality.

Simultaneously, the other Wave of Light is passing through us, expanding our awareness and our understanding of *who we are*, of who we have *always* been. This understanding is not located in the analytical, rational mind. It is centered in our broader field of perception within our knowingness, within our higher consciousness and the internal guidance system found within our heart. As we are beginning to remember *who we are*, we are beginning to let go of *who we are not*. And although letting go of *who we are not* is very desirable, letting go of our beliefs, our thoughts, and our concepts of the world may not be an easy, comfortable experience.

Memories of past experiences that influence our daily lives are often coupled with old emotional baggage that adds no value to our new *present time* creations or desires. All those old arguments, embarrassing moments, and painful experiences are stored unconsciously within our memory. They have nothing to do with who we are *now,* and thus have no value in the present moment. Yet we continually project those old attitudes and emotions into our future:

> "I will never talk to her again."
> "I will always be a failure."
> "I am poor."
> "I can't trust anyone."
> "I am not okay."

What your ex-partner, mother, father, teacher, minister, and ex-boss thought of you or said ten years ago has nothing to do with you *now*. However, what you place your attention on is what the Universe will lovingly provide for you. Continuing to carry the emotionally charged memories of past events only restricts and reduces your new *present time* choices. Fortunately, our multidimensional Higher Self knows that these charged memories have no further value. As we shift our awareness from third dimensional linear time to fourth dimensional *present time*, those memories that have no value to our growth and well-being dissolve, creating the awareness that we are losing our memories.

Because one of the two Waves of Light is expanding the range of possibilities within each of our realities, new choices are now beginning to replace the beliefs that were never yours. In simple terms, the format, structures and framework of the thoughts we think and the emotions we feel are changing. We are now shifting from a third dimensional to a higher fourth dimensional consciousness (and we will later accelerate further into a fifth and sixth dimensional experience). However, most people on the planet are not prepared for this Shift. Nonetheless, it *is* happening. And for those who are unaware of what's going on, it will not be an easy or comfortable transition. Look around you. With very little effort, you can observe those who still argue for their limiting habits and hold on to past events that are no longer relevant.

The creation of Heaven on Earth is unfolding before us, although it is not fully obvious because of the noise and fear surrounding us. We are at the threshold of a *new* beginning of life, not the end. But each of us must awaken *now*. Each must make the shift within. Many are awake and more are showing signs of waking every day, while countless numbers are still fast asleep—but not for long. We will each experience becoming aware in our own unique ways. For some, it will be powerful and alive; for others, it will be slower and more cautious, but we all will walk a path to wholeness. The ability to know yourself consciously in *present time* is now becoming available to you. Your purpose is to love yourself, enjoy yourself, and remember your Self.

CHAPTER TWO

Mastering Alchemy
And Creating Your Own Heaven on Earth

Alchemy is not magic; however, it does produce very wonderful and magical results. When you are aligned, Alchemy is the Universal Wisdom that nurtures creations into tangible reality. It is the Science of Spirituality. It is the dance that weaves the universal elements into conscious form. In short, Alchemy is the ability to transform one possibility into another.

By first accepting and then understanding that all things are possible, you are then able intentionally to transform one possibility into another. By simply learning to change one vibrational thought, feeling or belief into another, you will begin to understand how to create and sustain abundance, joy, and well-being. Alchemy is not difficult. In fact, Alchemy is much, much easier than you might think.

So what is Alchemy and how can you learn to master it?

If you wish to have water to drink, you need a container in which to hold it. If you have no glass, the water will quickly spill all over the table. Likewise, to hold the wisdom of Alchemy for your creations, you also must have a container. This container has long existed but has fallen away from us due to neglect, and to the fear that surrounds each of us. This container for the wisdom of

Alchemy is the electromagnetic field around you that you know as your aura. The problem is your aura has lost its definition or structure. You have become the water without a container.

By restructuring the harmonics of your aura to a particular sacred geometric form, you can recreate the container. This specific geometry aligns with a unique, higher dimensional body of wisdom and becomes your antenna—the receiver. The aura without structure and focus is like a radio that cannot tune in to the station you wish to listen to. Instead of listening to a broader, more distant station with many choices, you can only tune into the local neighborhood gossip. By creating a specifically tuned transmitter and receiver you can begin to align your personal energy field to your own frequency, which in turn allows you to tune out incoherent frequencies that constantly flow through you. These disruptive frequencies don't belong to you and have nothing to do with *who you are*, but they hold such a strong magnetic charge that they actually blind your understanding of your purpose.

Once this geometric container is in place, fascinating new opportunities become available to you. For example, by learning to increase the speed at which the geometric field spins, you begin to rise above life's dramas, noise and distractions. This creates an opportunity to realign your antenna to your own purpose and become happy. You are then consistently and successfully able to hold higher thoughts and feelings of passion, enthusiasm, clarity, and ease.

Your range of reception and awareness also expands, enabling you to tune into many levels of higher dimensional consciousness. This is much like upgrading the technology of your radio so that you are able to tune into and enjoy a greater range of music and news. All that is required is *the intention and desire to know your Self.* And a few simple tools.

As this occurs, you begin to recreate your Personal Power Field, which is the vessel that holds the wisdom of Alchemy. This is all the wisdom that is required for you to transmute the lead of ignorance into the gold of personal awareness. By fine-tuning your geometric field, or antenna, you will eliminate the noisy, incoherent vibrations of events and people around you, and begin to know yourself.

This fine-tuned alignment provides a new, quiet focus, which enables you to begin to remember and rewire your Self in ways that have not been available to you for many lifetimes. This allows you to recall, receive, and re-experience the abundance and wisdom that you already know in the higher dimensions. There is no anxiety, competition, worry or drama, because those energies simply do not exist within this geometry. You find yourself becoming certain, strong, clear, and non-reactionary. You have the ability to choose to listen to others, and then choose to experience yourself in your own way. Rebuilding your Personal Power Field restructures both how you perceive yourself and how you present yourself.

And here's where the magic really begins.

From this new, higher, faster perspective you will find that time exists in a very different form. There is no past or future. There is only *now*, where time is simultaneous and where all experiences exist at the same moment in the same place. Everything simply, effortlessly flows. In this simultaneous *now*, *all* answers to any questions are available to you *before* you have to act or respond to the question. The answers you seek exist exactly where you ask the question.

Think about this! If you knew all the answers, and what would happen in each situation before you had to act, then why would you ever choose an experience that was not enjoyable? With total choice, you would choose the possibility that most joyfully meets your needs and then step into that choice, thereby creating the reality that you desire.

From this higher, faster, clearer platform of consciousness, you will discover that many of the concepts, beliefs, and truths once held in this lower consciousness are no longer accurate or useful in the higher perspective. You now have the opportunity to make new choices. You can choose to play the game you have always played, or you can step up to a greater platform of certainty, seniority, personal power, happiness, command and grace. On this platform you will find that you have many more colors on your palette to choose from. The pictures you paint with this palette will be much grander and more alive. And by simply reconstructing a sentence or speaking with a different tone, you will create experiences with very different results. By changing the frequency of your thoughts, altering the harmonics of matter, and applying the element of Love, you will now be able to create and experience your dreams.

If this sounds like wishful thinking or fantasy, it is not. It is a simple doorway that has been hidden by the noise of the game—the push and shove, the right and wrong, the good and bad of the third dimension. You are about to step through a doorway that leads to merging with the Soul, walking with the Archangels, learning to create with the great Rays of Creation, and much, much more.

It is time to awaken and become who you are—a citizen of the higher dimensions. As the veils of ignorance and forgetfulness are being dissolved, many wonderful teachers, leaders, and healers are awakening. And as YOU awaken, it will be your opportunity to awaken others who are now stirring.

Alchemy is your natural state of wisdom. And mastering Alchemy is the means to create Heaven on Earth.

CHAPTER THREE

Understanding the Game of the Third Dimension
And How to Play It

With some basic information about what the Shift is, and an understanding of what dimensions are, *everyone* has the ability to evolve their consciousness and move gracefully and joyfully into these higher vibrational realms.

If you don't know what dimensions are, you are not alone. Have you ever played a game without knowing the rules? How did you do? Most people playing the 'Game of Life' as we know it in the third dimension are playing without having read the rulebook. The rulebook offers a conscious understanding that explains the Game and how one plays it successfully.

As previously discussed, we are stepping out of a third dimensional reality, passing through the fourth, and are on our way to the fifth dimension. Let me explain what the third, fourth and fifth dimensions are and why they are very important to this Shift.

If you can understand the structure and rules of these dimensions, you can begin to move fluidly through the unprecedented changes of this Shift without fear, without effort, and without the tension and anxiety we hold as the daily habit of our lives.

So first of all, let me define what dimensions are *not*.

Dimensions are not places or locations, and they are not a linear progression—3, 4, 5, 6—stacked up like pancakes. In general, dimensions are states of consciousness that are available to anyone who vibrates in resonance with the specific frequencies inherent within each dimension. In a way, you could think of each dimension as a different game with a unique set of rules about what is and is not possible for those who choose to play that game or create in that dimension.

These dimensions or levels of consciousness all have their own characteristics, and ways of thinking and feeling. Understanding the aspects, rules and structures of the third and fourth dimensions gives us the opportunity to step from the noise of the third dimension and its rigid structures into a more fluid set of choices held within the fourth, where we can then better choose where, and how, we want to live.

In order to make this simple, let's consider the third and the fourth dimensions each as a box. These two boxes overlap one another, allowing us to move from one box to the other. We have actually been living in the third and fourth dimensions simultaneously for well over sixty years. One box holds noise, rigidity, and uncomfortable emotions, while the other box holds choice, beauty, well-being and appreciation. You have experienced yourself in both these boxes. But without a clear definition of what occurs in each box, it becomes difficult to understand and master yourself even in the best of situations. By knowing the difference between the two boxes you *can choose* to live the life you wish to live, rather than simply *reacting* to life as it arrives on your doorstep each morning. By describing the characteristics of each box, we can develop a better understanding of how to choose.

The third dimensional box

First, the Earth, the mountains, the rivers, the lamp, the chair and the objects that surround us are *not* the third dimension. These are aspects of form. Form is the result of density. Form has shape, mass, texture, and weight—qualities that exist in both the third and the fourth dimensions. Consider that each of us is the lead actor in our own play. Form is the staging and backdrop that allows us to experience our play in physicality. Now here's a useful piece that is not obvious. Form is also held within our thoughts and our emotions. Although they are not seen as physical density, thoughts that are heavy or ugly will produce a response. Additionally, light, airy, beautiful thoughts will also produce a very different feeling or response. For example, have you ever accepted someone else's opinion that you've done something 'wrong', or are to blame for something, and then found yourself walking around with a heavy uncomfortable feeling of guilt? This guilt or blame is called a thought form. How you choose to observe and hold that thought form will influence your state of mind, your emotions, and even your physical health. It also determines your ability or inability to create your life successfully.

The third dimension is a box of rigid beliefs, with a relatively inflexible set of rules and limitations. Because most of us have been playing this game for lifetimes, we tend to think it is the only game or box available to us. But nothing could be further from the truth.

Understanding our third dimensional experience

The third dimension is very dense and operates within a specific set of rules and structures that hold many vibrations of thought and emotion. One of those vibrations is known as fear. In our spiritual quest to fully explore *All That Is* we went deeper and deeper into density, choosing to incarnate many times upon the Earth. We chose to go deeply into this density to experience who we truly are, and what life and living is all about. We, as enthusiastic spirits, wanted to know and to experience everything possible—and we still do today. Now, however, you may be asking yourself, "What could I have been thinking back then? Why would I ever want to try to live in this density?" But the higher parts of you were thrilled with the opportunity to explore and experience this dense newness. You actually jumped up, ran to the front of the line and yelled, "Send ME!" when the Creator asked for volunteers. We all did.

To maximize our third dimensional experience, and get an even bigger sense of abundance, contrast, and our individuality within this third dimension, we chose to forget the higher aspects of ourselves, and we lost our sense of connection to the Creator. It was as if we jumped into this game with a big bag over our heads to passionately play at discovering ourselves in this new world, with very little memory of who we truly are and where we came from. With this limited perspective and perceived sense of separation, we lost our way and, like abandoned children, we began to experience the energy called fear. This state of fear created further rigidity and limitation, making it more difficult for us to move freely and comfortably through life. As we continued to explore and play in this rigid third dimension, we began to take on many uncomfortable attributes, such as dis-ease, victimhood, guilt, loneliness, lack and resistance. As odd as this may sound, you chose to do and experience all this in order to know yourself better. And, in spite of what you may think today when you look in the mirror, you have been very successful at playing in this third dimensional game.

Fear is the most powerful emotion-charged thought of all. Fear is cohesive, solid and very real in the third dimension. It is perhaps the densest thought form. Fearful thoughts are super-charged with emotion, and these emotion-packed thoughts are like powerful magnets. They transmit signals to the Universe and the Universe automatically responds. If fear is incorporated in your point of attention, and in your belief system, it will unquestionably hold you in a third dimensional reality. You will not be able to move into the higher dimensions until you change those attention points. Becoming conscious of your fearful thoughts and feelings will disrupt the hold of the third dimension. Unconscious beliefs and repetitive habits will begin to release so that new choices can become available to you. Then fear simply becomes another choice, not a given result.

Many who cling to fear have created a default system or a box that gives them a false sense of security. "If I just go inside my house and close the door, I'll be safe." This reaction has closed down our ability to expand and grow, re-merge with our Soul, and remember our Higher Selves. Too many humans have stopped living their passion as they argue for their limitations within a web of fear.

The third dimensional matrix and structures

When we explore the composition of this third dimensional world a little further, we see three structures of this playing field or 'game board'. Understanding these will allow our transition through this grand Shift of Consciousness to occur more comfortably. Understanding the rules of the game will help you play it more successfully.

1 – Duality

Living within the field of duality was simply meant to provide us with a broad array of choices and opportunities so we may 'know ourselves'. Duality is a predominant structure of perception. Before the Fall of Consciousness, a long time ago, the purpose of duality was to assist us to learn how to walk in balance while experiencing contrast. If everything were blue, there would be no contrast. Once red is introduced along with the blue, we now have contrast. Contrast was created to provide us with experiences for choice, such as hot and cold, large and small, bright and dull, etc.

As we began to experience fear in our third dimensional consciousness, we added in to duality the concepts of right and wrong, good and bad, and should and should not. When we lived in the higher fourth dimension and above, there was no good and bad or right and wrong. There was no judgment, separation or competition. There was nothing to fear, resist, or argue about. There were just simple choices of contrasting opportunities, which gave us more ways to experience and know ourselves.

But with the Fall of Consciousness came fear, judgment and separation. We learned 'us and them', and we learned to resist and reject 'them'. These concepts of judgment, separation, good and bad, right and wrong and should and should not, created a rigid, unforgiving structure that does not allow for *flexibility* or *choice*. This third dimensional belief system bound and restricted our thoughts and emotions, creating a structure that was very conditional with extreme beliefs in 'never' and 'always'—rigid thought forms with very little opportunity for change, ease, or well-being. Fear and pain became anchored in this rigid belief system of heavy thought forms. This is what one of the Waves of Light is beginning to neutralize and remove from our memory as we prepare to step into the *present time* moment.

To assist in this adventure, the Creator made the Law of Attraction available. Just like a compass, this unwavering law reliably shows us where we are and what we are experiencing at all times. As we resisted our fears, a greater range of duality came about, and with our attention on the uncomfortable experiences, these fears magnified. We resisted this discomfort, storing many of our fears in our unconscious mind where we would not have to look at them or deal with them (we hoped). But the Law of Attraction doesn't just bring us the good stuff. It responds to the loudest, strongest feelings and thoughts we broadcast (those holding the greatest emotional charge) whether they are conscious or unconscious, comfortable or uncomfortable, desired or unwanted. Hence the saying, "What you resist, persists."

2 – Reactionary *present time*

One of the most rigid and unquestioned third dimensional beliefs that affects and structures our lives—our thinking, feeling and actions—is *linear time*. *Linear time* is the belief that time, and therefore our lives, flows in a certain pattern of past, present, future… and then we die. Because this belief is the default assumption of mass 3D consciousness, and events appear to validate this group agreement, most of us think and act as if it's true. However, it is incorrect.

Third dimensional time was not created as a straight line of events with a beginning, middle and end. It is actually a time-loop consisting of past and future, with a single insertion point known as the present moment, where we make new choices based upon past experiences and future desires. When we began reacting to life's situations with the emotion of fear, we began making fear-based choices. Our decisions about the future now became based upon the painful past, and our 3D life became a series of reactionary experiences founded in resisting what we feared, rather than allowing what we desired, thereby dragging the past with us into the future. However, because of the linear nature of the third dimension, time is perceived as a straight line from the past to the future. And because the Law of Attraction will never object to, or challenge, what we place our attention on, but simply deliver what we ask for, many of us waste a great deal of our energy ensnared in an endless cycle where our past haunts our future, and our future echoes our past. This time-loop becomes a flow of thoughts and experiences, which we label positive or negative, and connect emotions to. Either we embrace these experiences and hope they happen again, or we resist them and hope they do not.

In the third dimension there is a small sliver of the *present time*, known as 'reactionary *present time*'. In reactionary *present time*, we step into the future that we have created by resisting what we fear, and then find ourselves reacting to what we strongly, emotionally swore we never again wanted to experience. In short, we take our past experiences and project them into our future. We then step into that experience in a future *present time* moment to feel it all over again in a different size, shape, or color. We have planted the seeds of our future experience and what we draw into it by our emotional charges and reactions to our past and *present time* situations.

Let me give you two examples. First, let's say that as I am growing up, I am told by the wise and loving grown-ups that if I become a lawyer, doctor, teacher or nurse, I will be successful and have a happy life. As a child, however, this scenario does not feel correct in my internal guidance system, in my gut. However, I have no words or permission to disagree with the grown-ups and no logical reasons to help explain why this picture doesn't feel good inside. So I agree or simply go along with the plan. I take that past information from the grown-ups and place it out in front of me. I follow that belief into the future and live by it, *unquestioningly*. I go to college, get a degree and a debt, get a house and a spouse. I create the life the (now long gone) grown-ups told me I should in order to be happy. But I'm not.

Second, and this is perhaps a more important example, let's say that I once had a relationship that was the best of the best… until it was not. My lover left, telling me I was a terrible person, I would never succeed, I was not nice, and I did not have anything to offer to create a successful relationship with her. I was hurt. I felt rejected, and I went into a deep state of grief. Although I tried to get over the experience, I could not let it go, nor could I understand how I could be such a terrible person. Eventually I made the decision that I was okay, at least on the surface, and I never, ever wanted to meet someone like that again, because I did not want to ever be hurt again. So I scream to the Universe, "God, never let this kind of experience happen to me again. If a person of that type ever comes anywhere near me, please warn me and put up big red flags so I don't get hurt again."

Can you see how I took an uncomfortable experience from my past and placed it squarely into my future like a big, bright neon sign, and then added a large dose of super-charged emotional pain, fear, and avoidance in order to protect myself? And because the Universe and the Law of Attraction adore me, and it is the Universe's passion to satisfy my every request, guess what I found on my doorstep the next morning… and the next, and the next, and the next? With each step into the next *present time* moment, I experience precisely what I ask for through my vibration, even though it was the opposite of what I wanted. In other words, if the vibrations of my thoughts and emotions are negative, I get precisely what I put my attention on—more negative experiences. "Because you are the creator of your life and have free will to create your life in any manner you choose, I will provide you with exactly what you ask for," the Law of Attraction smiles kindly.

Also built into the structure of third dimensional time is a wonderful mechanism that can keep us out of trouble in this adventure. We have a buffer, which gives us the chance to reconsider the consequences of our reactive thoughts and emotions before we act and create something we might have to clean up or apologize for later. What we think does not manifest instantly. This buffer is created because in our distracted and noisy 3D life we don't keep our attention on our intention long enough for the thought to manifest into form. Our attention is unfocused and bounces from here to there so quickly that our desires don't get the amount of attention necessary to manifest. This built-in buffer allows us a moment of consideration before the next action. For example, the boss says, "I am so mad at her. I'm going to fire her." Then he shifts his attention and focuses upon the broken copier. Because our thought doesn't manifest instantly, we have a buffer period in which to calm down, reconsider, and avoid a potential mess. As this Shift is accelerating, however, this buffer is getting shorter, hence our thoughts and attention points are manifesting faster than ever.

So—to review: third dimensional time is not a structure; it is an *application,* or a tool, that allows us to create a new set of experiences based on our past, to be experienced in our future. This is how time works in the third dimensional box. As we move into the higher dimensions, however, our experience of time becomes quite different (and empowering).

3 – The rational mind

Most of us perceive our 3D experience predominantly with the left hemisphere of the brain, the home of the rational mind. When we came to play in this life adventure we disconnected approximately 90 percent of our brain and much of the body's energetic systems in order to have this experience. Thus, most of us are operating on about ten percent of our full brain capacity. The development of the rational mind served us well in this environment. Its purpose and job is to keep us safe and help us fit in. But due to fear and misuse, the rational mind operates more in limitation than in possibility and opportunity. We have also asked and expected the rational mind to perform tasks and participate in activities that it was not designed to manage. We've come to depend upon it far more than necessary, and to such a degree that our intuitive, creative, right brain, has become neglected and underdeveloped.

We came to play in this 3D game with the full potential plus all the necessary equipment and wiring to be fully conscious in all the higher dimensions. But because we have given assignments to the rational mind that it was not designed for, our awareness and range of choices have greatly diminished. Our innate spiritual abilities and potentialities are at best, weak, at worst, completely hidden from us. While the logical, rational mind is a wonderful tool for measuring, comparing, and storing information, it only knows what it knows, and it doesn't know what it doesn't know. It therefore works tirelessly to keep us within a thin range of objective, logical thinking, and possibilities. For thousands of years the rational mind has kept humanity tightly focused in the safe, structured, solid three dimensional realm. And we, for the most part, have gone along for the ride.

This is now changing.

Most of us suspect the rest of our brain must do something but have no idea what it actually does and how it functions. In fact, what the rest of the brain enables us to do is function in the higher fourth and fifth dimensions and beyond.

It is critical for our well-being and personal evolution to understand and recognize these three structures or aspects of the third dimensional box we have been living in. Reactionary *present time*, duality, and the rational mind, are intricately woven into the fabric of the third dimensional matrix. If you focus on or try to unravel only one of the three, the other two intensify, creating more distraction and more pressure, until you reset your focus and allow all three to come back into balance. By becoming aware of these underlying templates from which the third dimension operates, you can begin to have the choice to step out of it. You can reconstruct and remember a significant part of yourself, thereby becoming free to move beyond the limits of the third dimension so that you can begin to experience the possibilities of the upper fourth dimension and beyond.

Everything in the third dimension is also very *conditional*. For example, 'unconditional love' does not exist in the third dimension. If you experience unconditional love, you have actually moved into a higher fourth dimensional consciousness. You see, we have access to both third and fourth dimensional consciousness, but most of us rarely step out of the well-tread habits of third dimensional thinking and feeling.

The third dimension also offers no possibility of *choice*. We don't intentionally *choose* our thoughts, feelings, and actions in every moment. That is a skill of the fourth dimension. Instead we *react* to the people, and the situations that pop up throughout our day from our unconscious beliefs and habits.

Now let's explore the elements of the fourth dimension.

CHAPTER FOUR

The Fourth Dimensional Matrix and Structures

As we begin to become more aware and conscious of being conscious, we also begin to experience options and choices that are not available to us in the third dimension. The components or qualities of the fourth dimensional box are very simple, but because we invest so much of our attention in the motion and noise, reacting to our past and worrying about the future, we place very little of our attention in the present. Because of this pull between our past and future, it is difficult to become quiet enough to hold our attention on the simplicity of the life that is before us.

In the third dimension, the Law of Attraction responds to the noise, motion and reaction we hold within us, giving back to us more of the same. By understanding and living the four aspects of the fourth dimension, we can interrupt all those largely unconscious, emotionally-charged reactions, and instead consciously choose the outcome we desire, thereby allowing the Law of Attraction to give us our new, positive desires.

1 – Present time

Learning to experience yourself in the present moment is the single most important choice you can make in moving forward on your journey. Have you ever had the experience of being completely focused on pondering something and suddenly realize an hour has passed? Some call this being in the 'zone'. In 4D, there is no 'hour'. There is simply *present time*. So, if you're doing something interesting and enjoying yourself, you're standing upon the fourth dimensional platform. If you're expending a lot of energy figuring out the past and worrying about the future, or if you are trying hard to fix something, then you have slipped back into the third dimension. The moment you bring worry, doubt or fear into your fourth dimensional platform, you instantaneously return to the third.

If you find yourself wanting to argue with, "Yes, but…" or, "But what about this, what about that?" then know that it's your third dimensional rational mind coming up with a set of answers to keep you safe. If you ask why, if you stay in blame, or if you look for answers from your past-time experiences, you will find that those old emotional patterns get stuck. Remember—the rational mind only knows what it knows; it does not know what it does not know. So when you get new information that doesn't fit its model, it will argue with that information, and try to adjust, bend, turn and twist it so it can make sense of it, and then repeat it back to you. The difficulty is, the fourth dimensional platform gives you access to your Soul, to higher aspects of your Self, and to your spiritual abilities, which allow you to see and hear on a grand scale. The smaller, rational mind can't get its hands around that because those aspects of *who you are* are far too big. Because it doesn't understand, the mind has to invalidate the information, and that argument goes back and forth in your head. If you can consciously choose or recognize these various aspects as platforms, then you can move onto the fourth dimensional platform and allow the expansion to flow without the argument.

The structures of the fourth dimension provide a greater sense of ease, possibility, and capability than those of the third dimension. For example, where third dimensional *present time* is a charged reactionary moment influenced by our past, fourth dimensional *present time* is a quiet *now moment*. The focus is only on *this moment*, what is happening *right now*. The truth is we only exist in the *now*, but most of us hold very little of our attention here. We are consumed by past experiences and projected worries. Ironically, because we don't understand the structures of the dimensions, this fear runs through our mental and emotional bodies and keeps us bound to the third dimension. Our physical bodies, on the other hand, *only* know *present time*. Bodies can't know 'yesterday' or 'tomorrow', and as conscious beings, aligned within the fourth dimension, we function absolutely in this *now* of *present time* awareness and attention.

In the fourth dimension, past and future time also change significantly. In the fourth dimension, the past is simply history without emotional charge. Yesterday's pain has no bearing on tomorrow. The information, knowledge, and wisdom gained from the past assist us in making better decisions about our current and future well-being. The future is an opportunity waiting to be fashioned in this *now moment* through choice. Yesterday has no bearing on tomorrow, other than that the information learned in the experience can be chosen to be applied to a present, or future, *present time* moment. The eternal present is all there is. You can still plan for future events using information gathered from the past, but the decisions become conscious, deliberate choices made in this present moment. While the future is an opportunity waiting to be fashioned, it is in this *now moment* that choices are made.

2 – Choice

In the fourth dimension you take back your power to choose. When 3D reaction is replaced by choice you have more *flexibility*, which creates expanded opportunity and a greater ability to combine possibilities to produce a variety of outcomes. You are able to observe any and all events with a sense of detachment, simply as information to consider. From that still, uncluttered platform you are then, and only then, able to choose your response. In the higher fourth dimension you become *response-able*.

Conscious choice invites a wider range of possibilities, allowing for well-being, happiness and realignment with your truth. Fourth dimensional conscious choice gives you the opportunity to make mistakes and then correct the situation without blame or guilt. If you can allow what is in front of you to simply be what it is, you can then determine how you want to experience it. You can create the outcome you wish, or simply let it go. Choice. You make better decisions from the 4D platform of focused clarity, certainty, and an awareness of your own personal presence.

As the third dimensional good and bad, right and wrong fall away, an ever-expanding sense of capability begins to reawaken within you. Choice creates opportunity. Opportunity allows for well-being. Well-being awakens happiness, openness, and the *inner smile* within the heart. From your open heart, your purpose and the fulfillment of all your dreams are within your grasp.

3 – Paradox

As you become conscious of being conscious in this upper fourth dimensional reality, many higher concepts of life become available, allowing you to move around with greater ease and understanding. One of these higher concepts is *paradox*. *Paradox*, simply stated, is *what was true a moment ago may not be true in this now moment, and what was false a moment ago may no longer be false in this moment.* *Paradox* provides a flexibility to all those rigid, third dimensional absolutes, like *always*, *never* and *impossible*. It allows for flexibility and provides room for choices to be much more fluid and mobile. It also presents more opportunity. You are no longer locked into *always* and *never,* or "that was true yesterday so it must be true today." *Paradox* offers us more possibilities to release judgments, and increases our ability to allow. Instead of applying rigid, pre-existing definitions to any experience, we choose our preferred version and vibration in every moment.

Because of the fears, pain, and distrust that we all have stored in our unconsciousness, we hold many rigid beliefs about the world around us and those who live within it. We hold these beliefs anchored in words such as *always* and *never*. He will *always* be untrustworthy. She will *never* change. I will *never* forgive them. As the past pains of the third dimension are dragged into the future, our tendency is to react the same way this time as we reacted the last time, thereby repeating the experiences of the past once again.

As we consciously recognize that we have choices about the world around us, incorporating the concept of *paradox* allows the past to stay in the past, and frees the present and the future for new opportunities. *Paradox* allows us to recognize a person or situation as it occurred in the past; however, it now provides the opportunity to observe that person or situation in this unique moment, remembering the information of the past, but not engaging with the emotion of it. This allows them to be who they are now, rather than us observing them through the filter of our judgments, rigid definitions, and the limitations of our past reactions and charged emotions.

As *paradox* loosens up the rigidity of the past, the higher concept of *allowing* opens up broader opportunities for you to experience. *Allowing* is a powerful concept; it does not imply weakness, or inability, but rather, simply enables you to view the situation before you objectively, and provides you with a *present time* choice to create a better opportunity for a desirable outcome.

4 – Alignment and balance

The reality that we know as the third dimension is a classroom where we have been participating in the ever-expanding evolutionary cycle of our spiritual growth. In order to play in this classroom, we had to forget ourselves and leave much of our wisdom and knowledge, as well as many of our great skills behind.

In short, the third dimension is a classroom of *imbalance*. Your purpose, or mission, is to rediscover and master *balance*.

By balance, I don't mean your ability to walk or run without falling down. Instead, this is a balance and alignment between the totality of you in physical form, and *who you are* in the higher levels of consciousness. This is fully aligning yourself with your truth. However, since by definition the third dimension is *imbalance*, balance can never be found in the third dimension. It can only be found by stepping *out* of the third dimension. And this doorway is the fourth dimension. In the fourth dimension, we are constantly adjusting and moving towards balance and re-alignment with who we truly are—a spark of the Creator.

Once you begin to recognize the many tools, skills, concepts, and opportunities the fourth dimension provides, you will begin to choose and create your life much differently. The baggage that you've accumulated over years begins to drop away and you can choose to step out of habits of reaction and restriction. Trust becomes a choice. The need to experience lack, weakness, fear and doubt fall rapidly away as the structures of the fourth dimension are understood and practiced. You don't 'heal' yourself; you don't clear away your baggage. You don't even look for forgiveness from others. You simply become who you have always been and demonstrate this new presence. As this presence is experienced, *all that you are not* begins to fall away. And since time is collapsing, and many of your memories are also beginning to dissolve and fall away, you will find that all your deepest, darkest secrets—all those things that you hoped others would never know about you—you cannot remember any more. They are simply gone.

This new platform that you are building, and starting to live your life by, is really not a single skill, like learning to close your eyes and hold yourself in a certain energy. It's a way of life, a living dynamic that you are remembering and beginning to flow naturally within. What we considered to be mere words in the third dimension now have a fuller, deeper meaning and a more rounded flow in the fourth. Words such as Happy, Certainty, Seniority, Presence, Capable, Gracious and Commanding are no longer intellectual thoughts, but rather, become important internal sensations and feelings guided by your heart.

These concepts can only be felt and lived in the *present time* moment. As you remember and re-own these feelings and sensations, you realign with the internal guidance system within your heart. And as other higher, more vibrant words and energies become internalized, felt, and demonstrated within your life, a transformation occurs in how you present and experience yourself. These words are more than mere concepts. They are Living Words. They are energetic building blocks that we will discuss in a later chapter. As you begin to wear and experience these words they weave together, like a well-tailored suit of clothes, creating a new ease and a brighter presence. You no longer give away your power. You now begin to choose and create the life you wish to experience from these higher vibrations.

This is our natural state of being. However, becoming conscious, aware, and holding a well-grounded sense of self requires a shift in our habits and beliefs. Since childhood, most of us have been invalidated in our third dimensional experience. We have not been taught, encouraged, nor often even allowed to make decisions from our own naturally balanced platform of certainty, trust, and passion. Instead, most of us have been taught to fear and mistrust the world around us. Consequently, we have not fully experienced who we came here to be.

As we move into 4D consciousness in *present time*, with the power of *choice* and *response-ability*, and the flexibility of *paradox*, the ability to alter the game to enhance our happiness and well-being becomes available. Well-being, beauty, the *inner smile*, appreciation, and love are all options here. Fear is also a *choice*—but it is a *choice* that will place us back in 3D reaction and limitation.

The fourth dimension is the stepping stone to the higher dimensions; it provides us with an opportunity for movement toward a 'higher way of life'—a life of community, cooperation, and co-creation. Interestingly, fourth dimensional consciousness will not be a long-term option after the Shift clears away the rigid structures of third dimensional consciousness. The fact is the fourth dimension is serving as an essential, but short-lived, stepping stone or vibrational platform from which we will all move into fifth dimensional consciousness. The fifth dimension is the target for planet Earth and all her inhabitants. It is impossible to predict when and how this move will occur, because much depends upon the conscious evolution of humanity. That evolution is now occurring faster and faster.

Although the fifth dimension is the target, the experience of the fourth dimension is *essential*. We cannot enter the fifth dimension directly from the third. All mental and emotional baggage from the third dimension must be left at the door to the fourth; we can only enter the fifth dimension after we have become *masterful* of our thoughts and feelings in the fourth.

In the meantime, some assembly is required.

What is the fifth dimension?

The fifth dimension operates, to a great extent, in a completely different fashion from the third and fourth dimensions. Time in the fifth dimension is *simultaneous time*, meaning that everything (all possibilities) occurs in the same place at the same moment. In 5D, you focus your attention, and the answer is given where the question is asked. Ask and you shall receive. You don't have to move or go anywhere for your answers or experiences; everything comes to you easily and effortlessly based upon the attention point and vibration you choose to hold *in every moment*.

When you are vibrating in fifth dimensional consciousness, you don't create with form as you do in the third and fourth dimensions; you create with light patterns and light frequencies. You apply sound, color and geometric shapes. You consciously interact with the Creator and all the Beings of Light. In this heightened consciousness, the rational mind plays a very minimal role. It returns to the smaller, specific focus it was designed for—namely, analyzing and organizing thought.

There's much more to discover about the fifth dimension, but for now, the most important thing to know is that before we can move into and live in fifth dimensional consciousness, we must first become masterful of the vibrations and the possibilities of the fourth. Becoming masterful within the fourth dimension, and in our daily lives, is the purpose and the focus of the Shift as we move through the rapidly accelerating events of the next few years.

So—how do you become *masterful* in fourth dimensional consciousness?

CHAPTER FIVE

Mastering Fourth Dimensional Present Time

As discussed earlier, the fourth dimension is the 'right *now*' of *present time*. But *present time* actually has four distinct levels. Each level or strata of 4D *present time* has a shorter time-buffer than the previous one. For example, when we ask for an apple in the first level of *present time*, the apple appears in our hand after we find a ladder, climb up the tree and pick it. As we become more masterful and can sustain periods of quiet observation, and as we are less distracted by the noise around us, we begin to live in the higher strata of 4D *present time*. What we think is what we get at a faster rate.

Humanity has now stepped into and begun experiencing the third level of *present time*. Here our experiences accelerate, happening very soon after we think the thought. As we move through the next few years, we will step into the fourth and final level. In that level of *present time* when you think, *I would like an apple*, the apple will instantly appear in your hand. The time lag between your thoughts and your experiences will be eliminated. Usually when I mention this possibility, people get very excited. And it would indeed be exciting to have the ability instantly to create what you think. However… there is a however.

To manage the ability to quickly create exactly what you think, you must be extremely masterful of every thought and every emotion in every moment. How many times have you had a thought like the ones below?

I just know my car will break down.
My heart is broken and I feel like dying.
I wish she'd never been hired here.
He's going to kill me if he finds out.
I'm scared to death of snakes.
I can't see without glasses.

If an un-masterful thinker has the power to create every thought, there would be a trail of death and destruction in his wake. The vast majority of people are not masters of their every thought, feeling, and action in every moment. In the fifth dimension, not being masterful is not an option. We are required to be master thinkers and feelers as a prerequisite for entering the fifth dimension.

One of the reasons the third dimension was created was to provide us with a 'playground' in which we each can safely practice and hone the vibration of our thoughts and feelings without causing big problems. As we discussed earlier, to accomplish this, the third dimensional playground has a time buffer. Instead of instant manifestation, we (thankfully) have had a time lag between the thought we think and the manifestation or experience of that thought. If we didn't have the time buffer, learning to be skillful would be much more uncomfortable.

For the most part, humans are very sloppy with this buffer. Instead of focusing on the fun and positive things we desire and allowing this to unfold over time, we spew anger, frustration, boredom, worry, anxiety, blame, guilt, fear—all kinds of lower, disharmonic thoughts and feelings. Most of us behave as if we can think and feel anything with impunity because we don't see the instantaneous results of our thinking. We throw the negative energy, walk away and let others clean up the mess.

But not for much longer!

As third dimensional *linear time* is collapsing into a single point of *present time*, the time buffer is quickly collapsing too. We have less opportunity to practice being aware of and skillful with our mental and emotional habits before *what we think is what we get*. This is a very big deal. 'Practice makes perfect' and in this case, practicing is of utmost importance.

Fortunately, some simple, solid energy tools exist that can help you manage your thoughts and emotions in every moment so that you can be prepared for the unprecedented gifts, opportunities, and challenges of living and creating in *present time* in the higher dimensions. These fundamental energy tools will be covered in depth in Section II of this book.

Allowing the Shift to clear your unconscious thoughts and feelings

As mentioned earlier, one Wave of Light frequencies is coming onto the planet and clearing away your unconscious habits of thought and reactionary emotions associated with *who you are not*. As this occurs, all the lesser thoughts and feelings you hold *will* come into your awareness, and in turn can magnetically draw to you the people and circumstances that match these noisy, chaotic energies. There are two possible ways of handling this influx of lesser, yet powerful, energies. The way most in the third dimension react to negative thoughts that bubble to the surface is to reach out and grab the thoughts and energy that are passing by, and engage with guilt, anger, resentment, rationalization or worry. *Oh dear, why did that happen again? Why did I do that? I'm such a stupid idiot. That guy is a big fat jerk.* If you continue to engage or argue with this noise, these energies will not be cleared from your space, but rather will accelerate ever faster. These lesser energies will become consciously more uncomfortable, more consuming, and more damaging to your physical health and emotional/mental/spiritual well-being.

A better choice in dealing with these often powerful and overwhelming energies when they appear is simply to *allow* them to continue to move through and past your awareness. Simply observe these disturbing thoughts and emotions with a sense of detachment as if they are rolling past you on a movie screen. They are moving and coming up to be released, and they will neutralize and clear quickly if you refrain from grabbing at and engaging with them. Allow them and they dissolve. Soon, you won't even remember what the fuss was all about. If you can add some amusement to the act of observing, the speed at which the noisy thoughts and emotions disappear will be even greater.

Remember, most often what comes up is not even yours; it does not belong to you. Acknowledge it and know that it's coming up and leaving... *forever*. Take a couple of deep breaths, go for a walk, listen to music—turn your attention point to something (anything) of a higher vibration. Allowing your unconscious habits of thought and reactionary emotions to simply be what they are, instead of defending or fighting with them, creates the room and flexibility for that noise to continue to move up and out. Allowing that energy to pass by as you stand amused and detached allows it to continue its exit and leave your experience. If another aspect of that energy ever returns, it will do so with much less charge, and you will respond to it with much more neutral amusement. Success!

Understanding the lower and higher fourth dimension

To simplify another important aspect of the Shift, let's imagine that the fourth dimension has only two parts to it: a lower fourth dimension and a higher fourth dimension. (This is not technically true, but it's a useful distinction.)

Have you ever wondered where thoughts go when you are finished thinking them? Whenever I ask this question, people look at me with a stunned expression on their faces. The notion that thoughts could possibly have an existence of their own after you've finished thinking them is something that few people have ever considered. You see, thoughts don't simply evaporate into thin air; they all go somewhere. That somewhere is the fourth dimension. They continue to live in either the lower or higher fourth dimension, depending upon their density, weight, texture, and emotional charge. Like attracts like, and all thoughts bond and cluster with all other thoughts of similar character.

Thoughts that are nasty, mean, negative, and vicious in nature feel dense and heavy. They gravitate or sink to the lower levels of the fourth dimension and lurk in what we would call nightmares and other disturbing dream states. How is this possible? Your emotional body and your astral body are the same body. When you lay your physical body down to sleep, you give a command and the physical body begins to go into rest/sleep and the emotional body detaches from it. The connections between the two are held within the acupuncture points in the meridian system. They act like magnetic docking points to hold the astral/emotional body and your physical body together. As you drift off to sleep, one by one they begin to demagnetize. As they do, you, the spiritual body in the vehicle of the emotional/astral body, leave the physical body and pass through the lower fourth then through the higher fourth dimension on your way Home to the etheric realms.

Every stratum in the fourth dimension contains a collection of all thoughts that have ever been thought that are of a matching vibration. So if, as you fall asleep, your attention or energy is in thoughts with a dense, ugly and rigid vibration, you will begin to get pulled right into that lower layer of heavy thoughts as you pass through. As we pass through each successive layer, there is a lesser charge to the magnetic/electrical thought patterns stored there. The higher you are able to rise, the less dense and heavy the energy of each layer. What makes this even more challenging in terms of our ascension is that these layers of thoughts are held within the emotional body of planet Earth as well. In other words, the Earth's emotional body is the repository for whatever thoughts we hold in our own physical, emotional, and mental constructions. And right now, the Earth changes that we have been experiencing, are a result of the Earth going through her own transition, and doing her own cleansing.

What about those lighter, happy thoughts? Light thoughts such as 'butterflies', 'children playing in the park', and 'flowers blooming on a warm spring day', have a simple, bright and airy vibration to them. Lighter thoughts like these don't linger in the third or lower fourth dimension. Instead, they live in the higher levels of the fourth very close to the fifth. In order for us to align and feel the higher vibration of, for example, Beauty, we must step out of the dense 3D consciousness into *present time*, which is a higher fourth dimensional space.

"Wait," you say, "I know beauty!" Yes, you do, because you are now living in both the third and fourth dimensions simultaneously. But how often do you deliberately align yourself with, linger with, or roll around in the *feeling* of Beauty? For most, Beauty is a fleeting moment—e.g., "Oh, that sunset is so beautiful… Now I have to go over there and fix my problem." Your attention point moves from the higher fourth dimension quickly back to the dense, dull third dimension with hardly a pause. This is because lighter, airier thoughts and emotions hold a soft, electromagnetic charge that is expansive and fluid. Their charge, and therefore their staying power, is less. They are so light they require more of a *present time*, focused attention to hold them in your awareness.

Heavy, ugly thoughts, however, can, and do, stay in your space for a longer period. They are super-charged and tightly wrapped in highly magnetic emotions. Their charge, and therefore their staying power, is far greater. These heavy thoughts are not only harder to clear than kind, gracious thoughts; they also securely bond magnetically to all other thoughts like them in the lower fourth dimension. The reason the magnetic charge on ugly thoughts is so much greater is because there is an aspect of fear that is held within all our spaces. This aspect, as small and inconspicuous as you may think it is, still has an extremely strong, magnetic, emotional charge which reinforces the habit of letting yourself become consumed and affected by lower energies. It's the dynamic of one particular heavy, unconscious thought form attracting all the similar heavy, unconscious thoughts to it. That thought is simply: *I am not okay*. That thought is generated by the external third dimension, where we have been encouraged to look away from our own internal guidance of well-being and instead believe what the third dimension says is true. This is why it's vital to become conscious of the thoughts you think and the emotions you throw into your vibrational soup.

While one Wave of Light is clearing out everything *we are not*, the Law of Attraction supports us if we choose to keep any limitations, judgments, denials, blame, guilt, or resentment that we argue for. These beliefs, however, become like heavy weights on a hot air balloon. They limit how far we can rise within the dimensions and our personal ascension. We must, therefore, develop the fourth dimensional skill to hold positive thoughts and energies like 'happy', 'admiration' and 'beauty', and consciously choose to make them part of *who we are* and what we experience daily. These vibrations don't exist in the hurry up past/future world of the third dimension where it's very difficult to pause, to be totally present and smell a flower.

Fortunately, the other Wave of Light is making this progressively easier. As we let go of the heavier energies of *who we are not*, the Light is rewiring us and stepping us up into a higher fourth dimensional vibration where lesser thoughts and emotions are much less significant distractions in our general experience. We start to live in alignment with the heart, and experience the vibrations and consequences of thoughts such as *I like me*, *I'm happy*, and *I'm pleased with myself*. Your alignment with your heart becomes a natural way of life because it already *is* your natural alignment in the upper fourth, fifth and sixth dimensions. In real terms, you cannot be *not okay*. Your natural state of being IS well-being.

Here again, however, some assembly and practice are required to remember yourself.

Each of us is one hundred percent in charge of this process. The more weight (lower vibrational patterns of words, thoughts, and emotions) we remove, the higher we rise into the expansive experience of the upper fourth dimension and beyond. We are then able to look past our boundaries and limitations, which were always just old, dense habits of the third dimension. The higher fourth dimension offers us a wider, calmer, and quieter platform from which to view our life and creations. In the upper fourth you have the ability and freedom to choose fear or worry and therefore drop back down into the third or lower fourth dimension. As you progress and become more and more conscious and masterful, you will indeed fluctuate between these states of consciousness and dimensions. For example, you will occasionally forget and find yourself complaining and whining. You will also more quickly become aware of any uncleared negative habits and actively choose to release them and replace them with something lighter and more in alignment with *who you are*. Soon, you will make a deliberate choice never to visit that dense, weighty habit again. And you won't. In fact, you won't even remember any other option. You will have let that memory dissolve, and you won't remember who you were back then.

As you begin to align with your heart, you will discover there's no reason or compulsion for you to choose an uncomfortable attention point that resides in the third and lower fourth dimensions. Choosing to vibrate in the upper fourth dimension is a natural choice because it *is* the language and vibration of your natural state of well-being. You must, however, move the stumbling blocks out of the way, consciously allowing that higher state of being to be your daily experience.

This is a choice we are offered in every moment of our lives.

As the Shift accelerates and time collapses, *everything* moves into *present time*, including every thought you think. While you may still choose lesser negative thoughts and feelings out of unconscious habit, you will immediately and fully experience and recognize that old familiar discomfort. This is why it's beneficial to practice when it doesn't count. Developing the ability intentionally to choose what you wish to experience, in *present time*, before it counts is critical—because the moment it really does count is not far away.

CHAPTER SIX

The Seven Layers of Thought

The difference between success and struggle is the degree to which we are aware of and manage our intention, attention, and thoughts. Your unconscious thinking creates just as powerfully and swiftly as your conscious thinking does. Unconscious thoughts are like misguided missiles, whereas intentionally directed thoughts result in precise outcomes.

As this Shift continues to trigger more of the *who we are not* to surface and move out, understanding the steps or levels that our thoughts transition through may prove helpful in managing them. We are moving toward becoming more masterful of every thought, every emotion, and every action in every moment. Thoughts occur at many levels of loudness, from the complete silence of knowingness to the screaming and arguing thought that bursts out of your mouth without forethought. Although there are many levels or layers of thought, let's keep it simple and talk about the seven distinctive layers available to each of us. As we do this, please don't get locked into these layers as rigid lines. There is actually a fluidity and flow between them. The flow from one layer of thought to the next is similar to watching the dawning of the day. For instance, you can't easily identify 6:30 am changing to 6:32 am by looking at the sky. The sun rises and the sky flows from darkness into light. A moment ago it was pre-dawn. Now the sun is up and shining.

First layer of thought

The first layer of thought is where we simply speak without considering what we are saying. We see this occur every day. The man in the airport just blurts out meaningless comments. The woman chatters away as if she has no filter. Seconds later, they don't even remember what they were talking about. Functioning in this layer of thought, a person generally is unconscious of being unconscious, and goes about their day in a default mode versus being conscious and intentional. Most of those who have not awakened spiritually live here, but even those who are more awake and self-aware still find themselves moving in and out of this layer of thought. You might make a project of becoming aware when you are in this layer. Notice when you make unnecessary comments, gossip, or contribute to a conversation that is noisy. When you begin to become conscious of this layer of thought, you will quickly begin to become aware of and uncomfortable in the unconscious babble that you may find yourself surrounded by or demonstrating. You will make better choices about how to present yourself, and the layer of thought in which you want to live. This layer and the next two operate in third dimensional past/future time.

Second layer of thought

This is the layer where you have conversations or arguments with other people in your head. You go back and forth in your mind about the situation and how you were right/bad/wrong/hurt, and you scold the other person about how they were wrong/bad/hurtful/stupid. Guilt and blame live here, along with resentment and revenge. All these thoughts can be very loud and consuming sometimes. Although not spoken, this level of thought also has a relationship to telepathy and clairaudience, because that conversation you are having in your head is very real in the moment and it *is* happening. Whether the person is next to you or a thousand miles away, the conversation is occurring. On an energy level, that other person can feel the energy you are throwing at them. This is also the layer where you really want to curse at the person standing before you: "You stupid person/idiot/jerk," but instead you smile pleasantly and continue to argue with them in your head. Like the first layer of thought, this one has a huge amount of internal motion to it. In both layers you are still *going to,* or engaging with the situation versus listening, or being still.

Third layer of thought

This third layer is where you figure things out, strategize, fix, and problem-solve. There is still a bit of motion here, and an internal, back and forth type of conversation, as well as a degree of engagement and emotional attachment. This layer is very involved in the rational mind's need to figure things out:

> *I tried three different things and know this next way won't work. How can I get this computer issue figured out before this deadline?*
>
> *Okay, I said hello to her, but she didn't see me. What do I do now to get her attention?*
>
> *What does that sign over there say?* (Eyes squinting.) *It looks so interesting.*

Although not as screaming and intense as the first two layers of thought, there is still a small amount of undisciplined focus here. It has more to do with figuring something out for yourself, however, than with engaging with another. Your mind is bouncing around trying to find an answer. There is a looking outward for the answer, versus taking a breath, becoming quiet, and allowing the answer to make itself available to you.

Fourth layer of thought

This layer is a place that we will define as pondering. It is being curious, and sitting back without being engaged in a situation. This is the first non-engaged, non-invested layer of thought—Curious: *Hmmm, I wonder how that will unfold?* Or *Where did that come from?* Or *What an interesting possibility*. There is no emotional attachment, judgment, or pre-definition of answers or possibilities. Many times you get into this easy layer when you are not stressed or are not being pushed on; when there are few external demands on you at that moment. You might begin to think, *Hmmm, maybe it's time to consider moving. I wonder where I would like to live?* This is a question without a defined answer to it. The question is open-ended. The answer appears where that non-charged question is asked. All you have to do is allow it and not 'move' from your thought to search for the answer. The answer and the wandering thoughts surrounding the answer then come into your awareness from the broader field of possibilities: *Well if I go to Portland, Oregon, I will have this experience, but if I go to Tokyo I will have that experience, and then I could always move down to Perth in Australia and have that.* The process unfolds by itself and you are simply watching the process from a place of neutral curiosity. In this layer of thought someone may say to you, "Have you considered Boulder, Colorado?" And you are open enough to allowing, without rejecting or judging the possibility—no opinion, just curious. This is a *present time* fourth dimensional consciousness.

Fifth layer of thought

This is the layer of thought where things really begin to get creative and quiet. This is where your consciousness begins to naturally and organically pull together many of the floating, curious pieces, combines them with the deeper, unconscious aspects of you and begins to organize them in such a way that you become much more conscious, focused, and capable with your innate knowledge. This layer takes the curious interest of the fourth layer (the field of possibilities), and brings it to your mental workbench to organize and become more real as a possibility. This is done not with greater thought or concentration, but with a greater quietness, allowing, stillness, and trust.

This is where *I wonder where I would like to move?* unfolds into *Yes, Boulder feels aligned, right, and good* with no effort or worry or figuring it out—no thought, but accessing an awareness as if you heard the words but cannot define the location. Living in this layer of thought is magical, although it isn't magic. It is inspired. Many artists and writers create when in this layer. The creation process just flows and the book or painting writes or paints itself.

Sixth layer of thought

This layer is similar to the great meditation where you find yourself easily sitting still for three hours in an awareness of *this is so good I don't want get up*. This is the extremely quiet place where you begin to access deeper fields of awareness. You begin to think (or better yet exist) without thoughts as words. This occurs because you are in the higher fourth and fifth dimensional fields of knowledge. You begin to have conscious access to the greatness that you are. It is in this space that you begin to have a sure sense of your powerfulness, your presence, and what you are capable of.

This is where a thought enters the physical from the non-physical. This is where the Rays of Creation truly begin to be used to arrange and rearrange all possibilities without any limitations. Although no thought is thought in words, everything comes effortlessly to you. It is in this layer of thought that much of the work of the Mastering Alchemy Level 3 Program is practiced. You begin to play in the fifth dimension, where time, space, and gravity all operate differently than is understood in the third dimension. This is the place that Alchemy occurs, where you begin to rearrange the frequencies of thought, change the harmonics of matter, and apply the element of Love in such a manner that, on your terms, you rearrange the molecules and instantaneously begin to produce in simultaneous time whatever you desire.

Can you make that happen in this moment? The answer is 'yes'—but not if the noise of the first three layers of thought is your habit. As you play at this and become more masterful, you will build more templates of clear awareness and create expanding platforms to stand upon and create from. These fifth and sixth layers are where you will live most of your day in greater balance and ease. From here, you can then do what is necessary to allow more Light to come into your body. You can build the unified field of consciousness, which becomes One with the field of possibilities. It is in this space that you begin to know yourself as the Soul.

Seventh layer of thought

The seventh layer of thought is indefinable. There are no words available to describe it. It is where the thought that thought you into existence and you think together. Now, if I were to skirt around the edges of that with some definitions, I could say that this layer is the place where you are in full relationship with your Soul. This may be unimaginable to you. Your Soul has a great deal to do with the creation of you; the Creator created you, but your Soul also created you. And when your Soul, within the higher aspect of the Creator, and you begin to think together in the unified field, you are no longer a third or fourth dimensional being. You then begin to play very consciously in the fifth, sixth, and seventh dimensions as a citizen of those dimensions.

At this point you still have physicality, but not a physical body, as you know it. You will have a body that is full of Light and is less physically dense. The Light Body is now becoming very available to each one of us, but in order to create it, expanded levels of Light have to be brought into your form through the mental and emotional bodies. And these bodies are where we hold the third dimensional density, resistance and resentment. This is where ugly thoughts and ugly emotions live. The predominant purpose of this Shift is for you to become conscious of being conscious and aware of being aware, integrating enough Light into your mental and emotional bodies to the point where you don't have those ugly thoughts and emotions, reactions and resistances. When you can clear that energy from your emotional and mental bodies, the mental and emotional bodies merge and become one as they originally were intended. You will begin to play, with great awareness, in the sixth and seventh layers of thought. You will begin to change the density of your physicality from a carbon-dense body that does not absorb Light to that of a crystalline nature of Light that will allow a very significant transformation of your physical body.

This is what begins to happen in that seventh layer of thought, but what I just described doesn't adequately speak to what is possible. There are no words, although we are getting closer to finding them. In the meantime, I hope this gives you a better sense of these layers of thought and a structure that will enable you to become more aware of your inner workings. As you become the quiet observer of your thoughts and patterns, the noise will lessen, and a stillness of understanding and knowingness will prevail. And THAT is precisely where humanity is headed.

CHAPTER SEVEN

A Simple Truth About the Law of Attraction

In order to fully understand all that is about to be said as we continue, it is very helpful to understand the Law of Attraction from a slightly different perspective. Now, you might say: "But I already know all about the Law of Attraction." But *believing* you know about the Law of Attraction and *living* the Law of Attraction are two very different experiences.

Within the Universe, there are many simple unwavering patterns by which energy and consciousness flow without interruption. One of those patterns is known as the Law of Attraction. This law works perfectly every time. It simply says: "What you put your attention upon is what you will receive." Clear, concise, and simple. Maybe what is more important is that because it is a Universal Law it is flawless. It provides you with what you place your attention upon every time, with no exceptions. The Law of Attraction is the foundation of everything you have ever experienced, and it is key in all your future creations.

However… there are a few things you want to know before you make your next request.

1. The Universe adores you and wants only the best for you.

2. Because you are a creator being and possess free will, the Universe will not interfere or second-guess your reasons for what you create.

3. The Universe will provide you with exactly what you ask for. However, it does not understand words. It does not understand 'please' and 'thank you' in English, French, or any other language. The Universe understands your asking, or your intention, by how you organize and hold your vibrations, consciously **or** unconsciously. In other words, the vibration and energy you hold and embody is what will be responded to.

4. The Universe does not understand "Just give me the good stuff." What you place your thoughts and emotions upon, the Universe will **provide** for you. If you amplify your thoughts or beliefs with a charge of emotion (negative or positive), you will receive more of the same in a quicker, stronger manner. The emotional charge is the fuel that manifests your thoughts and intentions.

These points are very important to understand. Do you wake up and vibrate at *WOW! This is going to be a great day*? Or is the Universe met with *What a rotten day. I am not okay, I don't deserve, I am not good enough. I hate my job*? Because, remember, how you hold those thoughts, emotions, and beliefs is how the Universe sees and provides for you each and every second of the day. You scream out loud, *Universe, I would like to begin wearing nice, classy, well-made clothes*, but your thoughts, emotions and beliefs say, *I don't have enough money, I'm too fat. I don't deserve nice things. I always spill on my clothes and make a mess. I'm such a slob.* Can you see the contradiction in the vibrations?

I am not okay and *I don't deserve* do not create much of a vessel or container in which to receive what your words are screaming. Choosing to step into 4D *present time* and upgrading the platform upon which you experience yourself will begin to create the vessel and expand the possibilities and the goodies that the Universe has available and ready for you to receive.

Your *attention* on your *intention*— using the Law of Attraction

Have you noticed that as you've been reading this you have been completely in *present time*? You were not thinking about lunch tomorrow, you weren't in work this afternoon, you were right here. The reason we are bringing this to your attention is because there is a secret to the Law of Attraction that few people understand. The way to uncover this secret is to start becoming conscious of being unconscious. This begins with paying attention to what you're doing now, what you are going to do, where you're going to do it, and how you're going to make it happen.

Everything begins with an intention.

"I would like to…" is an intention. It's a proclamation. We have intentions all the time. We have great wants, thoughts, desires, and great intentions, some of which we create, and many that we don't, mostly because we forget about them as soon as we've finished thinking about them. This is fine if the thoughts you have are ugly 3D thoughts like those mentioned above, but what about your desires and dreams? Today you have this great thought…

I'm going to create a new business, a new relationship, a new… whatever, and then a minute or so later you don't even remember that you had that intention. It has dropped completely out of your consciousness.

If you decide to get a new job, and you're very clear about it, you are being intentional. You take certain steps, and you follow through on them. If you're getting ready to eat somewhere, you intentionally focus on whether you want Mexican, Chinese, or Italian food. In order to make your decision, you narrow your attention down to an even finer focused point… *Chinese has too much sugar in it. Italian has wheat. I'll go for Mexican.* Thus, your attention point is more focused. As you choose the exact restaurant and dinner you wish to experience, your attention point is locked onto your intention like a laser beam. You can almost taste the salsa and chips. And if your passion and desire and intention are emotionally charged enough, it will be a 2-for-1 night, and you can bring your best friend.

The Law of Attraction therefore begins with a thought, coupled with an emotionally charged attention point, focused upon an intention—a desire. The key to this focus is intention and not *going to* the distractions. Many times when we think, and thus when we create, we have a tendency to be in motion. Our attention point moves about. We think this, then we think that, then we move over here and we focus on this other thing over there. Very soon we lose track of our thoughts and become unfocused on our original direction and intention. As we move randomly around between attention points we are moving away from ourselves.

Our Self, however, is a spectacular point of singularity. One point—no motion. All things exist in this point, and from this singular point we can create, adjust, and move things around, and manifest worlds. But if we are always moving, always looking for something else, we lose focus and are unable to follow a thought. The secret to leveraging the Law of Attraction to create what we desire lies in refining our ability to focus our attention upon our intention without *going to* the noise and distractions. It's so utterly simple and profound, yet because we are always in motion, we don't truly understand what it means or how to master it.

Reverse engineering the Law of Attraction

Okay, so you understand what's required to leverage the Law of Attraction to get the things and the life that you desire. Is it possible to use that law to understand how you got yourself in the uncomfortable place you now find yourself, and skillfully make a better choice next time? Yes, and this is where it's helpful to employ your rational mind. For example, I find myself in a stressful situation where there is (again), the pattern of being 'taken advantage of'. For the third time, I have hired someone who is doing a lousy job and is causing problems for my customers, and anxiety for me. Because I understand that what I focus my attention on is what I get, I can reverse engineer the Law of Attraction to identify the thoughts and emotions I hold that continue to draw this painful situation to me.

- What thoughts do I find myself thinking about this newest employee? *He can't be trusted. Is he really as capable as he says he is? I must keep my eyes open to catch him if he messes up. Am I being taken advantage of?*

- What am I avoiding? *I don't want to learn this new software. I'm not patient or capable enough to understand how it works. I don't enjoy working with others; they make me nervous.*

- What emotions are running through my body? *Expectation that he will make a mistake with the software and cause a big mess and we lose customers. Fear that I will be left with a mess I won't know how to clean up. Fear of my business failing. Shame over my naivety and willingness to let others make decisions and do 'it' instead of me.*

- Where else have I experienced these thoughts and emotions? *Growing up, I was the victim of bullies. As a young adult, I never fit in and had no friends. In my first business, my partner took the money and abandoned me, leaving me not knowing what to do. In my current business, I continually attract employees just like these people.*

Now you have greater insight into that painful pattern, as well as a few words and energies to work with:

Abandoned
Nervous
Taken advantage of
Victim
Not patient enough
Fear
Negative expectation
Not fitting in
Give my power away
Not safe

Naive
Distrust
Doubt of my own capability.

This is a huge step, just as it is. Identifying the uncomfortable situation you find yourself in means you are 96 percent of the way toward changing it. The next three percent is getting amused at what you have just discovered, and the final one percent is doing something (anything) different. As we move into the second section of this book, you'll receive tools that will give you the opportunity to dissolve the patterns of pain that, with the help of the Law of Attraction, you created for yourself.

Experience the power of your thought

Would you like to play with your thoughts and experience how powerful they are?

Here is an example of how a simple, focused thought can influence your body. Please read each instruction, then close your eyes and experience the effect.

1. Think of a lemon. Remember and focus all your attention on a ripe, juicy, bright and luscious yellow lemon. Imagine its color and texture. It feels cool to the touch and the skin is smooth with many tiny dimples. Really visualize the lemon. See its shape and color.

2. Now imagine cutting the lemon in half. Watch the knife slowly slide through it and notice the pulp burst. Notice the drops of juice squirt and roll down the blade of the knife. You can feel the spray on your hand.

You can smell its fresh, bright scent.

3. Now pick up one of the halves and scrape your front teeth across the open, juicy pulp of this lemon. Take in the full experience of the tiny pockets of juice bursting and exploding in your mouth. Feel the burst of clean, fresh flavor and the texture of the pulp.

4. Really be with this lemon. Fully taste it, smell it, and experience it.

Notice the response of your body. Are your saliva glands stimulated? Are your shoulders tense? Take a breath.

You were just sitting there, having a very simple, common thought and your body responded. What if you took the power of your thought and directed it, not at a lemon, but at your relationship, career, or your health? That thought, so clearly and powerfully focused upon the simple lemon, caused an effect in your physical reality. Your thought can equally affect anything else you direct it upon. What would you like to focus on?

The condition of your body, your business, and every aspect of your life is determined by the thoughts you think. Fearful, worrisome thoughts and archaic belief systems keep you locked into a third dimensional reality and make it impossible to maintain a sufficiently high enough vibration and state of awareness to move you into a fourth or fifth dimensional reality.

To create balance and become a masterful thinker, you must first identify and release the tired or even harmful thoughts that no longer benefit you, and then replace those thoughts with ones that do benefit you. Sound simple? It is. However, it may not be so easy sometimes because there is a huge wall of conditioning and habit that you are pushing against when you begin to take back command of your thoughts and your life.

You can disrupt your fear-driven thoughts and emotions and replace those limiting beliefs by consciously choosing to focus on higher thoughts and newer perspectives. Once you begin to choose where you place your attention, new choices become available to you, and fear simply becomes another choice, not a given result. Manage your thoughts and emotions and you become a Master Thinker. Become a Master Thinker and you will have what it takes to capably use and direct the Law of Attraction.

In the next section we will begin to give you tools, skills, and different choices to expand your ability to change your unconscious vibrations and habits in order to vibrate in alignment with your intentions and asking.

CHAPTER EIGHT

Alchemy:
Changing the Frequency of Thought, Altering the Harmonics of Matter, and Applying the Element of Love

Archangel Metatron describes Alchemy as "Changing the frequency of thought, altering the harmonics of matter, and applying the element of Love to create a desired result."

Alchemy is the way to transmute fear into Love. This is a way of living your life with awareness and intention, returning you to a conscious relationship with the Creator.

Changing the frequency of thought

As mentioned earlier, thoughts are electrical and emotions are magnetic. This is a very important concept. When a thought is coupled with an emotion, the combined energies become electromagnetically charged and amplified, and set in motion.

Let us explain it in this simple way. We have all seen those big junkyard cranes that lift up buses, trucks and cars and move them around. Effectively, these are composed of a block of steel, which has magnetic properties, hanging on the end of a chain. It's not magnetic itself, but when you take an electrical wire, wrap it once around the block of steel, and then plug it in to an electrical outlet, it becomes electromagnetic to the power of one. In other words, it becomes a magnet, albeit a weak one. But when you wrap that wire around the block of steel ten times, or a hundred, or a thousand times, the force of the magnet is increased exponentially. It's now a very strong magnet that holds a tremendous amount of power.

Exactly the same thing happens within us. Many of us have been taught that we have four bodies, a spiritual body, mental body, emotional body, and a physical body. When you are in a state of ease, feeling happy and unstressed, just enjoying the world around you, you are in your spiritual body.

Now let's say that you are walking down the street, enjoying the spring flowers, and someone comes up to you and says, "You have a very funny nose." The mechanics of what unfolds next could be something like this: You drop from your happy spiritual space into your mental body, relinquishing your seniority and ownership of yourself, creating a state of 'dis——ease' (long hyphen). You think to yourself (mental body): *I don't like this. That's not a nice thing to say. What do I do with this? Why did they say that? What does it mean? Is this something I should worry about?* You begin mentally to analyze and figure out why someone would say this to you, running it over and over again in your mind.

Instantaneously, without any conscious thought or awareness, you then drop into your emotional body, and the hyphen between 'dis' and 'ease' gets much smaller. These thoughts generate an emotion, which doesn't feel very good— *I don't like this; it doesn't feel good. I feel hurt. Maybe I'm not going to be liked. I'm not good enough. I'm not appreciated. I'm never going to succeed. Oh, my, this is a big problem.* And right there, the emotion of 'off balance' now has an electrical thought wrapped around it: *I am not okay. I'm ugly. What are they going to think of me? I'm never going to amount to anything.* And the more you wrap the thought, the more powerful the magnet becomes. The more you ponder, the more you give up your seniority, and the more uncomfortable you get. You become embarrassed, you don't know what to do with this feeling, you can't talk about it to your friends, and out of desperation to get this feeling and the thoughts that accompany it out of your field, you put it in a place of unconsciousness by burying it in a box called denial.

But as we discovered earlier in chapter five, thoughts do not just go *poof!* and disappear. They all get stored somewhere. In the meantime, those unacknowledged thoughts and feelings of *I have a funny nose. I don't like myself. I'm not accepted. I'm not attractive. I feel so ugly, I'm never going to succeed* are still alive and vibrating in your unconsciousness. That wonderful asset you have, your best friend in the universe: the Law of Attraction wakes up with you in the morning and says: "Oh, look, there's Jim. He must love this game of being the victim, feeling guilty, ugly, embarrassed, and not okay. He must love it because he continues to puts a lot of his attention on it, albeit unconscious attention, and because I love him, I will create more of the same for him to experience today."

How you hold your attention is very, very important because it draws to you exactly what you get. The longer you hold on to the unconscious *I'm not okay, I'm not okay, I'm not okay*, the more this belief continues to grow and affect your daily life. It continues to be fed by the Law of Attraction, and it continues to be experienced in both past and future time. You so strongly don't want this painful thing to happen again that you hold it out in your future, and paste a big red flag on it that says DANGER! The Law of Attraction then simply smiles as you step into your future and into your next experience.

To complicate this even further, it is as if these thoughts and emotions, which start out as tiny pebbles in a stream, begin to grow into stones, and then rocks, and then bigger rocks that sit right in the middle of your energy pattern. Do you remember that spiritual energy of ease, flow, beauty, grace, happy and elegance? It now has a big rock in the middle of it, disrupting the smooth flow of energy. With this big *I am not okay* sitting right in the middle of your energetic flow of well-being, the energy begins to spill over the banks of the stream, creating irritation, resistance, and inflammation in your physical body, until the hyphen completely goes away. Disease is now in all four bodies. Illness, disease and physical difficulties, never, ever begin in the physical. They result from a combination of denied emotions, thoughts, judgments, opinions and fears, which create a state of imbalance—and many of those destructive aspects are not even yours.

It cannot be stressed enough— if your reaction (emotion) to a thought is strong, the charge behind it increases. If your reaction is negative, it may result in an angry outburst (discharge of emotion), or you may react by becoming offended and withdrawn, allowing that emotional energy to build inside of you.

Here is another example: Let's say you're wearing a new outfit and someone says it looks funny on you. That thought hits your emotional body, you feel insulted, and—wham—you instantly react. Even if the person only meant that it looked like a 'fun outfit', you've already coupled the thought with an emotion, which generated a knee-jerk reaction. If you are in a fourth dimensional space of ease, however, and somebody says, "That outfit looks funny," you'd simply pass over the word 'funny', and attach no judgment or emotion to it. You would respond rather than react or overreact. There is no victim or victimizer in fourth dimensional consciousness. You've changed the frequency of thought and continued happily on your way. In real terms, what other people think of you is none of your business—your business is about your business. And that is to be balanced and happy. Manage your attention point, thoughts and emotions and there you will be.

Changing how you feel changes everything. If you choose to think higher thoughts and feel lighter emotions you will raise your vibration significantly, and you will not find yourself gravitating back into old repetitive behaviors and thoughts of the third dimension. Often, when you interrupt a long-standing pattern (break the circuit) the energy flows backward and forward along the timeline, changing the energy all the way back to the first time this painful thing occurred. The energy is reset to the *present time*, allowing you the room to move freely again outside the emotional box.

You can change the frequency of your thought and create a different result. If you hear someone say, "Gee, that looks funny on you," smile and step up your energy a little to a happier place, where you might say, "Thank you! Yes, I feel fun when I wear it."

When you change the frequency of your thought, you begin to apply the tools of Alchemy and transform fear and reaction into love and ease.

Altering the harmonics of matter

Altering the harmonics of matter is not complicated, but to be successful it is essential to understand and master the result of combining a thought and emotion, as we explored earlier. Learning to observe without reacting, and allowing your feelings to be more fluid and at a higher vibration, are also necessary to the process.

Rather than changing lead into gold, let's start simply. As mentioned previously, thoughts have density. Once dense enough, thoughts materialize. If you are continuously holding negative thoughts of *I'm not okay* (in some form or fashion), they will become dense, and soon drop into matter. Many times, they show up in the world of form as physical illness or emotional/mental imbalance. Other times, those 'densified' thoughts show up as uncomfortable events or situations. Therefore, changing those thought forms is the first step in altering the harmonics of matter.

When you begin to experience the fourth dimension in *present time,* and recognize that you have choice, you introduce *flexibility*. Now you have the ability to alter the thought, loosen it, add to it, and bring new considerations into the thought.

Changing the harmonics of matter requires changing the frequencies or tone of thought. As you begin transforming your version of that ugly thought—*I'm not okay*— this can be very challenging. It has taken many years to build and anchor this negative thought in your life, so be patient and allowing with yourself.

Here is a suggestion to accelerate your awareness:

Begin to notice how you speak, and the words you choose to use in conversation with others. By choosing words that feel better in your speech and in your mouth, you begin to become more aligned with well-being, as well as less restricted in your choices. Consciously choose more interesting words; words that feel good as you speak them. It will be the speaking of these words that will move you into the fourth dimension with ease and balance, and allow you to more artfully change the direction of conversations before they starting veering toward fear, worry and problems. This is a very enjoyable skill to develop.

Applying the element of Love

Love is an interesting and very, very misunderstood word in the third dimension. Love, in real terms, does not and cannot exist in the third dimension. Love is open-ended, fluid, expansive, radiant, and powerful. It is a feeling that lingers and holds your attention very much in fourth dimensional *present time*. By definition, the third dimension is rigid, restrictive, conditional and reactive. Love, as a feeling, and a powerful creative tool, only begins to be present and available to you in the higher fourth dimension. Love has no end. Love is Beauty, the smile within you, a fragrance. Love is the power that moves the wind and pushes the ocean wave. Love is what holds the planets in their orbits. But most importantly, Love is the creative expression within each of us that creates. Love has no sword and does not restrict or limit possibility.

As you become masterful at changing the frequency of thought from the heavy absolutes of the third dimension to the alternate possibilities and new choices of the fourth, you begin to find a joy within your heart. This carries the new possibilities into more enjoyable outcomes for all. This ever-expanding element of Love will begin to become conscious to you. When you begin to recognize and experience the higher forms of Love in the fourth and higher dimensions, you can then apply them to your creations as part of Alchemy.

So, what are the higher forms of Love and how can you begin to experience them? Like many things in the higher dimensions, there are few 3D words that adequately describe them. Beauty is perhaps the easiest example to begin experiencing and anchoring this Love. Beauty is a fourth dimensional experience. Though it is experienced using the five 3D senses of the physical body, it moves within and through the spiritual body. The sunset looks beautiful; the music sounds beautiful, etc. Beauty is an internal sense or feeling, rather than an observation. Higher forms of Love can only be accessed when you already exist in the higher levels of consciousness, and there are very few words to describe or represent this Love. Higher Beauty is a recognition and appreciation of the grandness of All That Is. And while it may occur while appreciating a lovely waterfall, it is not about what you see with your eyes. It is expansive and not physical. For example, have you ever had a moment where you felt expanded and part of everything—a moment of such unification that you were unaware of your physicality? Those moments, which can occur during a great meditation, or listening to music, or being in nature, are moments that you can remember, recreate, and anchor, in order to begin to experience and apply the elements of higher Love.

Creating your desired result

As you play and practice with these three aspects of Alchemy, you will create your desired result. You become aware of the way of life that is now available to you. You begin to trust and open your heart again. You become aware of that *internal smile* that resides within you. A huge awareness returns to you, and you begin to rediscover your connection with All That Is. You experience compassion, co-creation, and cooperation. You begin to find alignment and your *internal smile* begins to take over your life. You begin to rewire yourself and reawaken. You reclaim that bigger, grander part of *who you are.*

This is where the true magic of Alchemy lies—*in the re-creation of yourself.*

SECTION II

Tools to Rebuild Yourself

CHAPTER NINE

The Path and Purpose of These Tools

Now that you understand the imbalance that humanity has been, and still is, experiencing, the question is: "How do we unravel the energetic structures, belief systems, and unconscious habits that keep us repeating the patterns and experiences that do not serve us or create well-being?" The path to self-mastery is not about feeding the rational mind information, data and facts. It is about becoming masterful with the tools, stepping past the chatter of the rational mind, and embracing the *experience* of the work. In this section we will begin creating new choices. This is where you begin learning about and working with the fundamental tools that will help you discover who you have always been but have forgotten.

The purpose of the tools we share here, and the many others that are available within the Mastering Alchemy programs, is to help you understand and rebuild the wonderful Personal Power Energy Field that surrounds you, but has been forgotten. This is accomplished with a specific set of powerful, sacred geometry tools and applications. Understanding how energy is organized, moves, and is directed, is fundamental to your conscious growth. By rebuilding this energy containment field, and realigning the core geometry of the Octahedron, you create an antenna, or alignment, which will enable you to access the frequency of your higher dimensional consciousness, your Soul, and your Higher Mind.

THE PATH AND PURPOSE OF THESE TOOLS

This path has been specifically designed for those of us who wish to accelerate our personal evolution, also know as ascension. This path of greater awareness will assist you to:

- Clear the density from your mental body by neutralizing disempowering thought forms, habits and patterns
- Clear the magnetically-charged emotional patterns and conditioning from your emotional body
- Learn to observe the ever-increasing third dimensional noise and drama without being affected by it and without experiencing internal chaotic emotions and judgments You will ultimately eliminate all such noise from your life
- Establish a stable, new platform from which to actively create your desires
- Ease ascension symptoms you may be experiencing
- Remember *who you are* and what you came here to accomplish
- Leverage the power of the seven Living Words
- Access the Sanctuary within your Sacred Heart and create a conscious, intentional connection with your Soul
- Begin to know all that your Soul knows
- Develop your innate spiritual abilities such as clairvoyance
- Begin to see with your eyes closed
- Begin to recognize, balance, and utilize both your masculine and feminine, creative potential
- Shift from thinking with your rational mind to thinking with your Heart and acting from the wisdom of your Soul—and a great deal more.

Fully incorporating the tools presented in this section, and living from these specifically crafted platforms will allow you to observe and move within the world, while consciously choosing what aspects of it you wish to engage in. You will begin to understand the concept and reality of clearly being *in* the world but not *of* it. From this expanded point of observation you will begin to utilize your inherent skills of clairvoyance, knowingness, and your natural ability to communicate with both your inner wisdom and the universal intelligence.

Getting the most out of this work

Allow us to make some suggestions as to how you might best proceed with your work with these tools. First, be in no hurry, the slower you go, the faster you will arrive. As tempting as it might be to skip around, each chapter in this section has been constructed to build upon the previous one, so read and work with the information in chronological order. Get comfortable with each of the exercises before you step into the next. Practice and play with each tool, and make them very real for yourself. This information will be absorbed on a number of levels as you read and practice. Only a small portion of what is being presented is being seen and heard with your eyes and your ears. Return and review often. This is about having fun, and remembering how great you are, so be playful and be light with yourself. This is not serious work (although the results are seriously profound).

Remember, the rational mind only knows what it knows; it doesn't know what it doesn't know. As you move through this work, use your imagination and allow yourself to pretend, just as you did when you were a child. This will give you permission to

THE PATH AND PURPOSE OF THESE TOOLS

go to places that your rational mind will not allow you to go when you are being serious and trying hard to make it work.

This next concept may be very new to you: You cannot do this wrong. You cannot make a mistake; it's not possible. So be easy on yourself, and remember — *you are not learning something new; you're remembering what you have forgotten.* The key to absorbing and integrating these tools is *feeling* the work not *thinking* the work. As you feel and enjoy this experience, you will begin to think with the heart and not with your rational mind.

Because some of us learn by reading the words, and others learn best by hearing them, instructions for many of the tools are presented in two ways. At the end of most chapters in this section, you will find a URL and a QR code that can be scanned by an iPad or Smartphone. Both the URL and the QR codes will lead you to a special page on the Mastering Alchemy website, where you will find accompanying videos and MP3 files that expand on the information provided for each tool.

When listening to the online meditations and exercises, you may find yourself occasionally going 'unconscious'. What we mean by this is that you may 'space out', or realize your attention was somewhere else while listening. Or you may think you've fallen asleep. If this occurs, don't beat yourself up; there is nothing wrong with you. It's simply that the new energy you are bringing into your body is not integrated or balanced within you yet. This unconsciousness will pass. Be easy on yourself. As you realign with *who you are*, this new energy work will begin to become integrated within you. Allow it; don't be in effort.

The Personal Power Field is very real. It is a field that surrounds you, and moves within and through you. It has always been there, but you disconnected from it to come and play in your 3D humanness, and then forgot about it. This is an opportunity to rebuild the geometry that will allow you to reestablish, recreate, rebuild, rewire, realign, remember, and fully reconnect with your Self. This will give you the ability to both reconnect to the Creator, as well as realign with your Soul.

Are there any obstacles to success on this path?

Are there any obstacles to success on this path? Yes—but only because many of us have been trained into habits that do not serve us. These habits will be revealed as you move through this book and listen to the accompanying online exercises. Below are some of the more common habits that you may notice. If you find yourself engaging in a habit, don't worry about it, and don't make it a problem. Simply notice what you notice, and make a different choice. Each new action is cumulative. This is the process of mastery.

Getting distracted by too many questions

Many of us are good thinkers and have a tendency to ask questions that really have no value, but instead contribute to our distraction and noise. Begin to notice when you challenge things with questions such as "Why is that?" "What does that mean?" and "How come I have to do it that way?"

If you can begin to practice what is called quiet observation, you will soon discover that many things are happening in perfect order. They are just not your 'old, familiar' perfect order. The thinking process has great value, but it does not have the ability or the wisdom to direct you on this path you are now exploring. See if you can turn your analyzer off while learning and practicing these tools. You'll benefit much more if you do.

Being in reaction

Many of us see or hear things and immediately, and often unthinkingly, react to them. We make assumptions based upon the expectations we have. Throughout these exercises, you will be asked to see what is in front of you without labeling, naming, or even identifying it. As you begin to master this process of *not going to* you will find that much exists right in front of your eyes that has been obscured by the judgments, assumptions, expectations and labels you have been taught to apply.

As you implement these tools, you will become more conscious of and let go of these judgments, assumptions and expectations. Many of those *I'm not okay* emotions that you have held for many years, will dissolve and disappear. When or if you hit these emotional places again, it will be helpful to remind yourself that these patterns are either on their way out and leaving, or are coming up for you to consider releasing. Do not grab hold of and argue with them. Simply allow them to surface then shift your attention to something that brings you to a place of feeling good (petting the cat, viewing a beautiful scene, smelling a rose, etc.).

Going unconscious when you close your eyes to meditate

Many of us have the habit of going unconscious when we close our eyes to meditate. This is part of an old pattern that simply no longer needs to be nurtured. In most of the exercises that follow, you will be able to open your eyes and close them while remaining fully aware and conscious. If you find yourself in the habit of going unconscious, however, you might try returning to greater clarity by opening your eyes, shifting your body position, or stretching, then closing your eyes again. This will begin to disrupt that pattern.

Have the intention to remain conscious as you work and be easy on yourself if you drift off. There is more information on this dynamic in the final section of this book.

Quitting before you begin, or getting tangled in the rational mind

The experiences you will have as you play with the exercises that follow are most likely different from anything you may have experienced to date. Your rational mind will not understand what you are doing. Questioning and challenging yourself, and getting tangled in judgments of *I'm bad, I did it wrong, It doesn't work, I don't know what I'm doing*, are all part of the noise of the rational mind. Allow us to be very clear: you CANNOT do this wrong! It isn't possible. So be nice to yourself, smile at the rational mind, take a breath, and continue.

Believing you can't 'see' or that you are not clairvoyant

You are clairvoyant. Clairvoyance is one of your natural spiritual abilities. You see and intuit just fine. However, you may not understand what seeing clairvoyantly really is. Those old expectations and habits are still in the way. Plus many of us grew up in a culture and a family that told us to stop 'imagining things' or that our invisible playmates were not real. Most have turned off their clairvoyance. If you will allow yourself to pretend that you see; you *will* indeed see. Seeing occurs first within your imagination then evolves from there. Play, allow, imagine, and then incorporate these choices as new possibilities just for the fun of it. There is a chapter specifically on developing your clairvoyance in Section III. Listen to the recordings provided for you online, and practice often. You will soon surprise yourself at how much you actually begin to see.

Staying attached to old patterns of relationships

As you engage in this work, the new relationships you form will begin to be different from those you have had in the past. You may even lose some old relationships. This is because you are changing very rapidly. The more you can notice this for what it is and appreciate it, the quicker you will continue to alter old patterns and reference points. This will allow the others around you to choose to move forward with you as you stop playing the third dimensional games you played together. Some of your friends and family may indeed like the changes they see in you and join you on the path to well-being and wholeness. Others may choose to stay where they are. If they do choose to remain in the box of their limiting habits, allow them their choices. They will eventually arrive where you are, but until then your choice is to grow and know yourself. Only then will you demonstrate yourself as the radiant example of what wholeness can be.

Our invitation to you

It is now time to learn how to take back ownership of the Center of Your Head, rebuild your Personal Power Field, begin operating from the Higher Mind, and build a new platform from which to create your life. We invite you to play with the information and tools in the same way children play with building blocks. Children can become completely absorbed in seeing how high they can build the tower of blocks before it tumbles down around them. Then they begin again with curiosity and enthusiasm.

Explore and play in the same way as a child who is fascinated with music will spontaneously explore the possibilities of a piano. Browse, and allow your curiosity. Find something to play with and see where it leads. Put it down, pick it up, let it sit and settle for a while. Be the fascinated little child, unhurried and unworried, simply curious. Along the way of this path, you will receive information and choices to change the unconscious habits that do not support your well-being. The tools you are about to learn will help you recreate something that you unintentionally but very successfully gave up a long time ago.

Will it be simple? Yes.

Will this be easy? Kind of.

Does it require awareness and a choice from a *present time* space? Absolutely.

Can you sit on the sidelines and hope it all turns out okay? No, not any more.

If you use the tools that you learn, listen to the meditations that are provided free online, and apply yourself to the exercises offered, we can predict that, by the time you finish this book, you will have gained a new and far more expanded understanding of *who you are* and what you are capable of. You also will have created for yourself a solid foundation for becoming masterful at recreating your life, and shaping the world around you.

CHAPTER TEN

Tool # 1
Reclaiming Your Command Center, Finding the Center of Your Head

Discovering and understanding *who you are* requires that you bring yourself into a *present time* focus. This is not difficult, but some attention and practice is required.

There is a place within the center of our heads that acts as a command center; a place where clear decisions can be made and actions can be set into motion. However, as we grew up, we learned to give up this place and trust the opinions and beliefs of others. Many times our mothers, fathers, teachers and ministers said they had a better idea of life (and how we should live it) than we did. We learned to give up our power to their thoughts and beliefs. We stepped away, and relinquished command of our decision-making. But more importantly, for many of us, we stopped listening to our connection to our own internal guidance system. We gave up knowing our own truth and lost ourselves.

Because they wished the best for us, the mother-father-teacher-minister wanted to show us how to live and experience life—the right and wrong, good and bad, and should and should nots of life. They told us how we should behave, who we should be friends with, which schools we should attend, and what we should do in order to be successful. As a result, many of us heard and had the experience of being told:

"You are not doing it right. Do it my way."
"You're not okay."
"You don't deserve that nice thing over there."
"You are never going to amount to anything."
"You're not very smart."
"You shouldn't wear that."
"You're too clumsy."
"We can't afford nice things."
"I know what you need and want."
"You're so sloppy and messy."
"You're not very attractive." Et cetera.

Most of us have had the experience of the mom-dad-teacher-minister in our life saying, "I know better than you. I love you and I know what will make you happy and successful." They may have been subtle with that message, or blatant. Either way, many times this did not feel right, but we allowed their thoughts and truths to become ours, replacing our own inner knowing. Many times, instead of loving guidance, we experienced invalidation and control—"See only what I see. Do only what I do."

Remember, thoughts don't just disappear; they all go somewhere.

So where did many of those thoughts and commands from the mom-dad-teacher-minister go? To a great extent, they went directly into the center of your head, displacing *you*, moving *you* to the side—"See only what I see. Do only what I do."

TOOL # 1 - RECLAIMING YOUR COMMAND CENTER

We then began to view our world through the filters of their thoughts, their beliefs, and their experiences, rather than our own. We grow up, and the habit continues. We still allow others to get into the center of our heads and establish their values, preferences, and goals there. We continue to give up our seniority to the many others we associate with—our colleagues, spouses, and friends.

You can change this habit.

Before we give you a number of tools to re-own the Center of your Head, and return the energy of others back to them, let us ask you: do you know where the Center of Your Head is? Can you quietly and fully experience being and living within the Center of your Head? For most, the answer is no.

Is it possible, however, for you to begin to take back your power, own the Center of your Head, and ask everyone else to leave? Yes! It is the Center of *your* Head, after all. You are the owner. The others are just visiting—although they may not see it that way.

Let's begin. Here's a little exercise to help you locate the Center of Your Head:

- Place the index fingers of each hand on either side of your head, at the soft spot where your temples are.
- Close your eyes and imagine that you are drawing a line from one finger to the other. Observe the position of that line.
- Now, without losing track of that line, move your fingers 90 degrees. Move one finger to the center of your forehead, just above your nose. Place the other finger directly opposite, at the back of your head.
- Take a breath.
- Draw another line from each of those fingers, creating a

- line that runs through your head from front to back.
- Find the point where the two lines intersect and bring your full awareness to that point.
- Be at the point of this intersection. This is the Center of Your Head.
- Take another breath, put your hands down, and close your eyes.
- Now just *BE* at that intersection for a few moments. Notice what you notice, without labeling.
- Be comfortable right there. Relax, and be amused with yourself. Curious.
- Breathe. Get very quiet and still. There is nothing to do.
- Look through your closed eyes as if they were windows.
- Glance out at the room around you. Don't try to see anything, but be aware of yourself in the Center of Your Head. You don't have to be perfect at this.
- Look through your closed eyes and relax your body. Notice if you have been holding your breath, and resume breathing.
- Look around the Center of Your Head and create a special space there for yourself. Imagine a comfortable space you can easily spend your time (your life!) in.
- Take one more breath, and get a good sense of where the Center of Your Head is and what it feels like.
- Notice your body from the Center of Your Head.
- When you are ready, open your eyes, and be aware of the room. Notice if you feel the need to blink your eyes, and refocus. Smile.

Are you in the same place of awareness that you were just a moment ago? Does it feel different from where you were when you began the exercise? Most likely the answer is 'yes', because being in the Center of Your Head is not a place in which most people spend much time.

Now try this:

- With your eyes fully open, bring your attention back into the Center of Your Head, right behind your eyes.
- Breathing will help this very much, so take a smooth breath, and be right in the Center of Your Head.
- Notice if your body feels different in any way. Some people notice that their body feels a little awkward. Others say they can't put words on it, they just know it feels different. There is no right or wrong answer.
- Relax and continue to be in the Center of Your Head with your eyes still open.

Congratulations. This is the Center of Your Head. This may not seem like a big deal, but trust us, it is a huge deal and will become more so. Do this exercise a few times to anchor this awareness for yourself.

What you may notice

If, as you experiment here, you notice your attention has wandered from the Center of Your Head try this: lick one finger and touch it to your forehead. As the moisture evaporates, the coolness can keep you focused in your command center.

It's not unusual to experience occasional noise or mind chatter in this space. Those are the energies and voices of the mother-father-teacher-minister who are protesting this change in you. It isn't you. Think of it this way, you are changing the game. Everyone who has been in the Center of Your Head is now noticing, and they don't like the idea of being evicted. They grumble and protest, wanting to know why you are changing things around. You, the owner, are moving back in, and the squatters have to leave. If this chatter and noise happens to you, there are other tools we will provide you with to help you become more focused, and to release those distractions.

How would you like to live your life from this space in the Center of Your Head? How would you like to work from here, and have a relationship from here? Understanding *who you are* requires that you be in *present time*. Observing the outside world from the Center of Your Head offers you that *present time* point of observation and awareness. This is an energy space that is not restricted; it can be animated and very excited, but it is a *managed* energy space. This is where you begin to know yourself—right here.

As this Shift of Consciousness unfolds, the Center of Your Head is the location you will want to operate from as you begin to move from this third dimension to the fifth dimension. You are going Home. You are being moved, by your Self, from the dense third dimension to this higher state of consciousness. And everything begins from the Center of your Head.

If you would like to practice and become masterful at living life from the Center of Your Head, we have prepared two recordings that lead you gently through the experience of finding the Center of Your Head, using the circular breath, staying in the present moment, and not going into 'trance'. To access these recordings, copy the URL on the next page into your browser, or if you have a QR code reader on your Smartphone, you can simply scan the code.

TOOL # 1 - RECLAIMING YOUR COMMAND CENTER

www.masteringalchemy.com/mabook-tool1-center-head

CHAPTER ELEVEN

Tool # 2

The Gift of Grounding—
Whose Thoughts Are These Anyway?

As we have discussed, many of the thoughts you think and the beliefs you hold do not belong to you. As you begin to realign to your own personal frequency by re-owning the Center of Your Head, you can now clear away those thoughts and emotions that are not yours by rebuilding your grounding mechanism.

Whenever we talk about grounding, people often sigh and say, "Oh, I know all about grounding, I've been grounding for years." But when we ask them if they are aware that there are *two* elements to a Grounding Cord, they invariably look surprised. So in case you're thinking of skipping this section, stay with it. We will rebuild your Grounding Cord both electrically and magnetically, and you can see what happens.

Grounding is a natural part of the electrical and magnetic systems of the body. We are born with this cord, and all the other tools we mention here. However, in our third dimensional fear and concern, and in our moving between the past and the future, we have forgotten how to ground the body to make it safe. There are two components to grounding. Remember we said earlier that thoughts are electrical and emotions are magnetic? One component of your Grounding Cord consists of an electrical line that runs from your first chakra at the lowest tip of your spine, to the center of the Earth, which grounds non-aligned electrical thoughts—i.e., the thoughts that are running through your head all day long that have nothing to do with you. The second component consists of a coil of energy that wraps around the electrical grounding line, and also runs down to the center of the Earth. This is the magnetic portion of your Grounding Cord, and its purpose is to clear away all the emotions and uncomfortable feelings that do not belong to you.

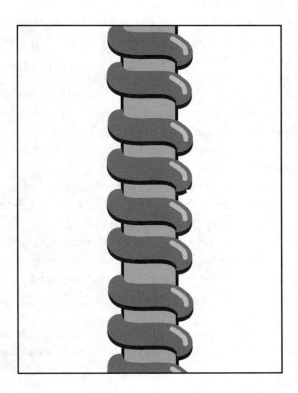

Here's an exercise that will give you a valuable experience of what it is like to ground properly:

Grounding Exercise

- Close your eyes and in your imagination create an image of a beam of Light, a line of energy, a tree trunk, a pipe, or a chain. Just pretend.
- Then connect one end to the lowest tip of your spine (the first chakra). *Feel* the connection. Make this real.
- Now drop the other end of the line to the center of the Earth. See the line of energy strongly connecting to the center of the Earth.
- Pretend (pretending is very important here) that you have an imaginary third hand, and reach down, tug on both ends and feel the connection. Really *feel* the pull.
- Expand the line to about eight inches in diameter and then give it the command to activate and become electrical.
- Give it the command to begin automatically to release any disruptive thoughts, known and unknown. Take a breath, notice your body, and relax a bit.
- Take a moment and as you continue to watch from the Center of Your Head, notice the thoughts that may come to your attention. As they do, you can firmly and gently guide them down your Grounding Cord.

To actively release the patterns of emotions that don't support you, we will now add the magnetic component of the Grounding Cord.

- Bring your attention to your first chakra again.
- Imagine another long cord or wire attached to your first chakra. Pretending works well here too.
- Watch as this coil automatically begins to wrap around the original electrical portion of your Grounding Cord. It may move quickly or slowly. It may be a color or not. It may wrap evenly or randomly. There is no right or wrong.
- When this magnetic coil reaches the center of the Earth, give it a tug at both the top and bottom to be sure it is secure.
- Give the command for this coil to activate and become magnetic.
- Then give it the command to draw to it all the unsupportive emotions you might have; those you may be aware of and those you are not aware of. Take a breath and allow your body and mind to relax a bit more.

Grounding allows destructive thoughts and emotions to simply siphon off down your Cord into the Earth, thereby minimizing the noise and disruption in your life. If, as you play here, you find old emotions and thought patterns surfacing in your reality, this is a good thing. Don't try to stop them, or argue with them, or ask why they are there. It's just the old stuff that is being released. You are reaching and clearing the deeper layers of stuck energy. It isn't important where it came from. Continue to use your tools and allow the energy to move out.

- Now shift your attention to something that's uplifting and be happy. As you do this consistently, you will also find these limiting patterns being dissolved from the world around you. Soon, you won't even remember many of those old patterns, because they are being cleared from your third dimensional time-loop.

As you practice and play with the Grounding Cord tool, you can also take the opportunity to clear any ugly emotions and thoughts that you have noticed in your experience recently. "Where in my space do I hold X (jealousy, fear, judgment, lack, and so on)?" Notice what you notice and allow that energy to also flow down your Grounding Cord and dissolve.

Although there are two components to your Grounding Cord, it is important to always activate both. Your thoughts and your emotions are interwoven in deep ways, and as you release one, the other begins to unravel. Keeping both parts of your Grounding Cord in place and activated allows the energy to be neutralized quickly. With your Grounding Cord firmly in place, all those troublesome, repetitive thoughts that don't belong to you, and all those charged emotions that get you unnecessarily stirred up, now have a place to go. You can now actively remove them from your space.

Copying and pasting the URL on the next page into your browser, or scanning the QR code, will lead you to a short video of Jim demonstrating the Grounding Cord at a seminar, along with an accompanying MP3 recording that expands upon the value of the Grounding Cord and how you can use it to clear your aura.

TOOL # 2 - THE GIFT OF GROUNDING

www.masteringalchemy.com/mabook-tool2-groundingcord

CHAPTER TWELVE

Tool # 3
The Rose

The Rose is the workhorse of these energy tools and one that even the most practiced among us return to again and again. The reason is the Rose tool can be used in many different circumstances. This tool will help you establish, define and hold your space while you move through the noise of the third dimension. Like a broom or vacuum cleaner, the Rose will remove the opinions of others that have accumulated in the Center of Your Head. Separating your energy from others is necessary for clear decision making and for recognizing your truth from theirs. The Rose does this most effectively. This simple tool will assist in gathering your energy up from where you left it during the day and before you go to sleep. It is also an excellent and efficient tool for releasing any limiting beliefs and habits that the Shift may be rising to the surface of your life.

Why a Rose? Why not a Turnip?

The Rose has a long cultural history of use in ancient mystery schools and in spiritual applications. In addition to having a higher and faster frequency, in physical terms, than any other living organic substance on Earth, it is a much loved symbol that has little to no negative charge. This, coupled with the fact that it has a natural Grounding Cord (stem), makes it one of the most powerful and valuable energy tools we can possess. When you take a slower vibrating energy and place it next to a faster, higher vibrating energy, the slower one is consumed; it loses its power and is no longer noticeable or influential. Imagine how a huge bonfire will cause the flame of a single match to pale in intensity. When you use the Rose, this same dynamic occurs with any type of energy, including the energy of belief patterns. Any lower, slower belief patterns, whether it is fear of escalators, or *I'm really dumb,* will be consumed by the brighter, higher energy of the Rose. Disappointment, for example, when surrounded by a happier thought quickly disappears.

A bit about the aura

The aura, or energy field that surrounds you, appears as an egg-shape. It has seven multicolored layers, each of which relates to one of your third dimensional chakras. The aura of a balanced person extends about an arm's length away from their physical body and radiates in every direction. The aura gathers, retains, and files every thought, word and action that occurs within, through, and around you. In other words, it holds a great deal of information, much of which has very little to do with you. Depending on what someone says to you or how you experience yourself, the energy of this field will change. It will become tighter and stiffer with negative, insulting comments or energy. If you are validated or given more permission to feel safe, your aura will become more flexible.

Think about some of the people around the world who have very fundamental structures, very rigid attitudes and very fixed ideas. When you look at such people, do they look as if they have flexibility? Do they look as if they have permission to experience themselves fully, or do they appear to be functioning according to a set of rules, most of which are not even theirs?

The aura was not designed to function as it does today. It was designed as a structure that held and stabilized the energy field, however, as we entered the third dimension we forgot it and allowed it to deteriorate to where it is today. This lost structure had allowed us to know ourselves in ease and joy, while allowing others the same freedom within their structure. When this structure was forgotten, we lost track of ourselves, and our sense of definition. Quite simply, we lost track of our personal space—i.e., where we start and stop, more or less. When we do not know where our space begins and ends, it's all too easy to take on other people's energy, thoughts, fears, emotions, and attitudes, and to believe that they are our own. Without defined boundaries, we allow people to get into our space all too frequently, and we get into theirs.

For example, many of us have been raised to believe that empathy and sympathy are desirable traits to develop. Because we all have a natural spiritual ability known as *clairsentience* (the ability to 'read' energy by feeling the emotions of others), it is very easy to fall into empathy and sympathy and feel the pain of others in our body. For many of us (especially the healers and nurturers among us), the moment we hear that someone is upset or unwell, we immediately want to 'fix' their problem. So we move in a bit closer to them, ask what's wrong, encourage the person to share more details, so we can really understand the problem, and in the process we align ourselves and our energy with theirs. We *feel* them and their problem. Before we know it, we don't feel so good ourselves anymore. We match that person's problem and their issue is now in our space, and we're feeling the effects of it too. When you don't have a point of reference for where you begin and end, you simply don't know where you are, and consequently you don't know whether you are reacting to your own emotions or someone else's emotions.

Interestingly, this happens to many of us all the time. We allow other people's energy into our own space without even being aware of it. They don't have to be physically close to us for this to happen. They can be on the other end of a phone, or across the planet from us. There are many vibrations and frequencies that are being broadcast all over the world all of the time, many of which, at any given moment, are a match to your own vibration and frequency. So think about this: when you're feeling off balance or depressed, and are wondering, *Why am I feeling this way? What's wrong with me?* Chances are it's not you at all.

Can you imagine how useful it would be if you could eliminate this habit and experience from your reality? The Rose is a tool designed for this purpose and more.

Let's get started and play with the Rose and experience what it can do.

Rose Tool # 1
Establishing, Defining and Holding Your Space

- Close your eyes, take a moment and find the Center of Your Head. Establish your Grounding Cord. Take a breath.
- Find a memory of a red Rose—perhaps it's one that you saw at a florist, or in the garden, or at the grocery store. Remember it just as you saw it. Allow yourself to see it.
- Without leaving the Center of Your Head, imagine yourself holding this Rose straight out in front of you about twelve to fifteen inches (30-38 cm). See it in your mind or imagination. If you find it hard to visualize, pretend.
- Now, keeping your imaginary arm fully extended, with the Rose firmly held between your thumb and fingers,

picture yourself turning 360 degrees, tracing a full circle around you as you do so.
- Take your time and become aware of yourself within this circle.
- Draw your full attention inward to your side of your Rose, and notice how this feels.
- Stay on your side of the Rose. This means holding all your energy and attention between you and the Rose. None of your attention is beyond the Rose.
- Take a breath, open your eyes and stay in the Center of Your Head, Grounded, and on your side of the Rose.

From now on, this circle that you have just created around you with your Rose will serve as your point of delineation. This defines your space. Your job now is to stay on your side of the Rose and within this circle. All that lies within this circle is you. This is where you experience yourself. All that lies outside your circle is Shakespeare's theater, the stage upon which others enact their plays for your amusement. Everything within your circle is your experience; everything beyond your circle belongs to others.

When you begin to observe your life from this vantage point, life becomes much easier, calmer, and smoother. As you now know, when you operate without a point of delineation, you become affected by the noise and drama of those around you. In other words, rather than living your own life, thinking your own thoughts and feeling your own feelings, your thoughts, feelings, and reactions are many times being dictated by the effect that others have upon you.

Speaking and interacting with others

As you go about your day and interact with others, keep the Rose at the edge of your aura. You will be able to have a perfectly normal conversation with them, as you talk through the Rose and simply allow it to do its job. If they move closer to you, simply adjust your Rose to stand halfway between the two of you, whether that is two feet or two inches. Once you understand and experience this, people can walk right up to the tip of your nose, and you will be able to maintain the same composed conversation with comfort, ease and awareness. They are on the other side of your space, not within it.

If the person you are speaking with becomes emotional or dramatic, the Rose will prevent this drama and pain from entering your field. You will discover that by staying on your side of the

Rose, you will experience a new feeling of neutrality. Putting the Rose between you and another person in a potentially emotional or contentious situation not only enables you to remain calm and detached from the situation; it also helps you become a much better listener. You will have the necessary clarity and ease to ask better questions, and to assist them when they ask.

Of course, the most effective time for setting up the Rose tool is prior to entering a conversation with someone. Remembering the tool while you're in the midst of a conversation works better than if not used at all, however, preparing in advance is always the wiser idea. Make this a game. Practice when it doesn't count. Practice at the grocery store, the gas station, and whenever you're engaged in casual conversation with friends or family.

How not to feel the pain of others

Besides allowing you to let everything that is on the other side of the Rose simply remain there, the Rose gives you a valuable moment to observe, choose, and then calmly and much more confidently act. This is the fourth dimensional *choice* vs. a third dimensional reaction. The Rose creates a delineation or opportunity, not a separation, which allows you to know with certainty that the distance from your heart to the Rose is your energetic space to experience the wonders of you, and everything outside the Rose is Shakespeare's theater to entertain you. When this is understood, you will find that your experience in relation to the pain of others is quite different. The purpose of this tool is simply to allow all of that theater to come right to the edge of the Rose, stop, be observed, and then either be chosen to be enjoyed, or chosen to be passed by. There is no reason to run the emotions of others through your body. This is a very effective tool that allows you to observe situations, and the emotions within them, without being affected *by* them.

For example, as we move through this Shift, many long established institutions are changing and crumbling. We're experiencing a global economic crisis, housing crises, and personal financial crises. You hear people talk about how they are losing their jobs and homes, or having difficulty paying their mortgages. While you may not have any difficulty paying your own mortgage, you can't help but feel the anxiety and discomfort of others as you listen to their sad experiences, or watch the evening news. You may not need a loan for your new business, or your new car, but as you watch, hear, and feel all the anxiety, worry, and problems in the third dimensional world around you, this energy runs through you and makes you also feel concerned and off-balance.

The Rose will enable you to walk through this intensifying third dimensional world without experiencing it. It will allow you to be in the presence of sadness and worry, but not part of it. You will continue to be compassionate and caring about the painful experiences of others, without running the fear of their experiences through your body.

Other ways to play with the Rose

- Place the Rose between you and the telephone during a charged or challenging conversation.
- Between you and the car behind you that is tailgating. To do this, first place it on your bumper, then slowly move it further behind you. Then watch the car slowly move away from you.
- Between you and a scary movie.
- Around your car before you begin driving.

- Around your home, office, or other space.
- Practice when it doesn't count so that when you want to use it, you will have developed a strong relationship with it. Play with and imagine your Rose in a variety of colors, levels of openness, with and without a stem. Practice moving it around your body and exploding it.
- Check in with the Rose at the edge of your energy field occasionally throughout the day and clean it off or freshen it up. Your casual attention to the Rose will refocus your awareness in *present time*, as well as strengthen your boundaries and keep you in your own space.

Placing a Rose around others is not as effective, however, as each of us is responsible for our own energy field and well-being. But you can always offer them the Rose tool for their own use, if they ask.

Rose Tool # 2
Clearing the Center of Your Head

By virtue of living in the third dimension, we have all allowed others into our space. The mother-father-teacher-ministers in our lives have well-established residencies in our physical, mental, and emotional bodies, as well as in our energy field, and in the Center of Our Heads. As mentioned previously, out of their concern for us having a good life, they have given us their opinions and truths, and we have agreed to accept them. It is time to give their truths back to them, where they belong. Until we give them back their energy, opinions, and truths, we are unable to live by our own.

The Center of Your Head is the favorite place where this energy and the untruths of others are placed and remain. It is therefore important to clear this space out regularly as part of your daily routine. In fact, we suggest you clear the Center of Your Head before you engage in any other energy work. Ground, find the Center of Your Head, and clear it out as part of finding your space and establishing it as your own.

Clearing bothersome thoughts from the Center of Your Head

- Close your eyes, take a few moments to find the Center of Your Head, and establish your Grounding Cord. Take a breath.
- Take a few moments to be completely focused in the Center of Your Head. A trick some people use is to imagine a room or outdoor space there that can be easily recognized and returned to.
- Create a Rose of any color within the Center of Your Head.
- Notice the first thought that pop ups and, from a state of neutrality, begin to direct it into the Rose. Allow the entire thought to flow into the Rose. The Rose may change color as this occurs. This new color represents the energy of that thought.
- Move the now full Rose outside of your energy field and explode it like a firework, allowing all of that thought to dissipate and leave your space.

Some well-established thoughts may require a few Roses to dissolve completely. Those are the thoughts that have lingered the longest and are the most valuable to move out of the Center of Your Head. If they return later, simply repeat the process. When you are ready, you can move on to the next exercise and learn how to clear people from the Center of Your Head.

Clearing people from the Center of Your Head

- Find your space again. Take a breath.
- Create another Rose of any color within the Center of Your Head. This Rose operates much like a vacuum cleaner, sucking up the energy, opinions, and thoughts of others.
- Without waiting for the image or thought of a person to pop up in your mind, begin to imagine moving the Rose around and through the Center of Your Head with the command and instructions for it to 'gather up all the people' who have left their opinions or truths there. The color of this Rose may change. This new color represents their energy that is being drawn into the Rose to be released.
- The faces, names or memories of others may pop up as you do this. Allow them to enter the Vacuum Rose without grabbing them or putting your attention on them.
- You may also ask the Rose "Who else is in the Center of My Head?" Observe without engaging or *going to*, and simply direct them into the Rose.
- You will have a feeling when the Rose is complete for this session. Move the now full Rose outside of your energy field and explode it like a beautiful firework, allowing all of that person's energy to leave your space and return to their own space, where it belongs.

You must remain neutral for this Rose vacuum to work. If you find yourself becoming charged or engaged, simply return to finding your space and begin again, or end the session and return later. Like the long-established thoughts above, there will be people who have lived in the Center of Your Head for a very long time, or in a very charged manner. It may take several sessions to fully 'decharge' their hold on you. Take your time. Be patient.

Who is that in your head?

There are two types of friends who may tend to occupy the Center of Your Head most strongly or frequently. The first are people with whom you are in a positive relationship, like dear friends and members of your family. It is just as important (or more important) to give them back their energy as it is to give back the energy of those whom you are not fond of. The Center of Your Head is yours and only yours. If someone you care about has left some of their energy in your space, they don't have access to that energy for their own use and well-being. It is a great gift to return this portion of your friend to them. This does not mean you care less for them, or that they will care less for you. Indeed, quite the opposite—clearing them out of the Center of Your Head allows each of you to see and to engage with each other more cleanly. You clear away yesterday's thoughts and discussions, so today's can be more clear and enjoyable.

The other type of friend you may find residing in the Center of Your Head is an animal friend. Like dear, human friends, your animal friends can place their attention in your space leaving less room for you. Give them back their energy just as you would give back the energy of your human friends.

Rose Tool # 3
Making separations from others using two Roses

In addition to holding the energy, opinions, and truths of others within the Center of Your Head, your entire aura, including your physical, mental and emotional bodies, also hold their attention. Return to them what is theirs, and you will have more room for you and your own goals and dreams. You may then create your life the way that suits you, rather than the way that suits them.

- Take a few private moments to find your space. Clear your mind and the Center of Your Head of any thoughts and people you notice there.
- Imagine or remember a white Rose. Place it about 12-15 inches (30-40 cm) out in front of your face.
- Begin simply—think of someone who is somewhat irritating to you, or gets into your space, or whom you just can't seem to stop thinking about.
- Visualize and pretend putting this person in the white Rose, and watch what color the Rose turns. This is the color of this person's energy in your space. This is not 'bad' energy; it just doesn't belong to you. The other person needs that energy back to feel whole again.
- Create a second Rose next to the first one. This Rose represents you. Notice the differences in color, shape, openness, etc.
- Give the command to the other person's Rose to collect up all of his or her energy, and its color, from your Rose. Watch as their energy and color leave your Rose and returns to theirs. Allow this to occur at its own speed. Soon, you will become aware that the Rose is complete.

Leave the Rose there.
- Now give the command to your own Rose to collect up all of your energy from the other person's Rose. Watch as all of your energy simultaneously leaves their Rose and returns to your own Rose.
- When both Roses are finished exchanging energy, move the other person's Rose outside of your space and explode it or make it disappear. Their energy will now return to and benefit them. Think of one thing you appreciate about them (a tiny appreciation is okay here).
- Now put your attention on your Rose again and allow it to enter your body. It is filled with your unique energy. Your Rose has the wisdom to know where in your space to return your energy to you. Let it fill you up.
- When you feel complete, breathe your eyes open.

Rose Tool # 4
Making separations from others using one Rose

This method works better for some people than the previous method, so we encourage you to experiment to see which you prefer.

- Prepare your space as described previously and imagine a single white Rose before you.
- Think of someone who you would like to make separations from.
- Visualize putting this person in the white Rose and watch what color the Rose turns.
- Imagine their Rose below your feet. Instruct it to rotate slowly around your body, collecting up all of this energy and color that is not yours from within, around, and

through your physical, emotional and mental bodies. The Rose can also begin at your head and spiral downward if you prefer.
- When their Rose reaches a point above your head, or below your feet, thank the person, and move their Rose outside of your space and explode it, giving their energy back to them.

Just like the technique of clearing the Center of Your Head, if the person whose energy you are removing has been in your space for a long time, or in a strongly charged manner, it may take a few Roses to release all of their energy from your space. Be patient with yourself.

Rose Tool # 5
Gathering your energy up from where you left it during the day

As you move through your day, it is best to collect yourself up from each situation or event as it ends and before the next one begins. This not only allows you to make room for the new *present time* experience; it also ensures that your experience of this new *present time* moment is not influenced by the past moments and the people you were involved with. When you don't do this, it is like ending a phone call with someone, and not hanging up the phone—the static of the last call continues until you hang up. By doing the following exercise, you will be complete with the first client before you go on to the next one. You also will be more present and clear in both your mind and your emotions, ready to offer them the best of yourself. Gathering yourself up is a valuable and important tool, whether you have a series of appointments or only a few consuming meetings during your day.

If we don't routinely gather ourselves up throughout the day, we leave portions of our energy (and attention) in the places that we have passed through. We leave a bit at the stoplight, at the store, with each client or co-worker, at the gym, and with the people we spoke with on the phone. Have you ever returned home from a long day to find you are still having a conversation in your head with someone you met? Not clearing out between appointments causes you to accumulate and collect every one of them in your space. By the end of the day, you will feel exhausted, uncomfortable and have no energy left. You will be carrying everyone you met and all the energy of those events in your space. Not a good thing. This is like leaving your money all around town. When it is time to take care of your own needs (i.e., purchase dinner), your wallet or pocketbook is empty.

The steps described below can be used throughout the day and as you prepare for your nighttime travels. Clearing out the energy of your entire day, and collecting yourself up as you sit on the edge of your bed preparing for sleep, will provide for a better night's rest. This will also allow you to pass easily through the noisy, distracting, lower levels of the fourth dimension (the astral) on your way Home each night. (Please see Chapter Five for more information on the lower fourth dimension and how we move through the noise stored there as we go off to sleep.)

Between daily appointments

- In a quiet place, take some breaths and find your space. Be in the Center of Your Head, Grounded, and within your energy field.

- Imagine a single Rose of any color and place it out before you.
- Give it the command to magnetically collect up your energy from the last appointment/event you participated in.
- Notice the images and thoughts that pass by your awareness without grabbing them or engaging with them. Just watch, objectively, as they come up, and your energy flows back into the Rose.
- You can ask the questions, "Who else did I leave my energy with?" "Where else did I leave myself?"
- Allow the Rose to do its job and collect up all of you. Notice what you notice.
- When the Rose has filled up and gathered all of your energy, the passing images and thoughts will have slowed or stopped. Your intuition will tell you when the session is complete.
- Be in gratitude as you draw the Rose into your emotional, physical, and mental bodies, and watch it returning your energy back to you.
- Smile and be pleased with yourself.

Gathering yourself up before you go to sleep

When you are finally alone at the end of your day, perhaps while sitting on the edge of your bed, take a few moments to find your space and breathe.

- Imagine a single Rose before you.
- Give it the command magnetically to collect up your energy from your entire day.

- Notice the images and thoughts that pass by without grabbing at or engaging with them. Watch as they come up and your energy flows back into the Rose. You'll be surprised to see all the places you left your energy. Be amused at yourself.
- You can ask the questions, "Who else did I leave my energy with?" "Where else did I leave myself?"
- Allow the Rose to do its job and collect up all of you and your energy. It may move around your space. Take your time. You will want to be as clear and whole as possible, before resting.
- When the Rose has gathered up all of your energy, the passing images and thoughts will have slowed or stopped. You will know when the session is complete.
- Be in gratitude and draw the Rose into your four bodies, watching it return your energy to you and filling you up with *who you are*.
- Have an intention of what you would like to experience on your journey Home tonight—e.g., deep, peaceful rest, communication with angels, etc.
- Crawl into bed and smile.

Rose Tool # 6
Releasing limiting beliefs and habits

The heavy, dense programming of the third dimension will not allow you to rise to higher levels of awareness and consciousness. The *I'm not okay* in its various forms will keep you stuck in the third dimensional box of limitation and drama. It is, therefore, an absolutely necessary requirement to begin and to continue to free yourself from the limiting beliefs and habits so you may live on the higher platforms. This is the entire focus of this work. Using the Rose tool for this objective is one of the most simple and effective ways of proactively releasing your baggage and *who you are not*.

You can utilize this tool at any time, during any meditation or working session. It is also very effective to use prior to an event that you know may trigger an old habit, fear, or limitation. For example, before you find yourself in a situation that has previously inhibited or paralyzed you in any way—public speaking, an important meeting, standing up for yourself, going on a date, etc. This procedure works equally well when you recognize other habits in your life, such as competition, fear, jealousy, or victim.

Practice when it doesn't count

When you discover yourself in a situation where you are uncomfortable or overwhelmed by the charged energy flowing through your body, remembering the Rose tool will completely shift your experience. Most of us, however, are unable to remember much of anything when in such charged situations. When we are stuck in the energy, we are stuck. Don't wait until you are in a situation to use this tool. It is easier, more fun, comfortable and effective to do the work *before* you find yourself in a charged situation. Put your parachute on *before* you jump out of the plane.

- As always, get yourself into a quiet, noise-free place. Find your space.
- Imagine or remember a white Rose out in front of you.
- Think of a limiting belief or habit that you know affects your life.
- Place that belief in the Rose before you. Watch what color the Rose turns. This is the color frequency of the charged

habit or belief in your space that you are about to de-charge.
- Give the command to the Rose to collect up this color and belief from wherever it may be lodged in your space. It may be stuck in any or all of your bodies, or in your energy field.
- Spend a few moments simply sitting in the Center of Your Head, watching this Rose do its job.
- It may move around and through you, or it may simply work from a stationary position in front of you. If you choose, you can actively move it around your space.
- You will notice images, memories, or people pass through your awareness. Allow them to keep moving and don't analyze them.
- You will know when the Rose has collected up as much as it can during this session.
- When it is full, visualize moving the Rose outside of your energy field. Explode it, or imagine it zooming off into the atmosphere. The point is to imagine it completely disappearing and dissolving from your space.
- Congratulate yourself. You have released another layer of limitations and baggage. You are another degree closer to fully living on a higher dimensional platform.

This is a process. It took you years to get to where you are today, so be patient with yourself. Sometimes when you are releasing other people or beliefs from your space, uncomfortable memories or feelings may surface. Sometimes the physical body experiences sensations. This is a normal indication that the tools are working for you. The more you can remain neutral, in the Center of Your Head or your Higher Mind, and Grounded, the quicker that discomfort will be dislodged and released. If you find you become too charged and uncomfortable to continue at any point, don't resist it. Simply call it a day, and return tomorrow to peel away another layer.

This isn't a race. Be in no hurry.

You can enjoy more energy work and meditations with the Rose tool on the web page that you can access using the QR Code or URL below.

www.masteringalchemy.com/mabook-tool3-therose

CHAPTER THIRTEEN

Tool # 4
Your Higher Mind

In third dimensional terms, the Higher Mind is located an inch (2.5 cm) up from the Center of Your Head and an inch and a half (3.8 cm) back. It is a place of stillness and is much more expansive than the Center of Your Head. It is in the Higher Mind that you begin to become aware of *all that you are* and all that you are a part of.

It is here, in the Still Point of the Higher Mind where all information can be found. The Higher Mind is vast. It is quiet, and there is a detachment from the world around you. There is focus, clarity, and curiosity, but no questions are asked. It is through the Higher Mind that conscious contact with your Soul begins. It is from here that access to the heart becomes available in a manner that is totally unapproachable from the noisy third dimension. Third dimensional words are inadequate to describe the state of awareness and ease that accompanies living from the Higher Mind. There are many important opportunities that arise by observing life from this vantage point, but none is more important than your reconnection to your Soul.

Finding your Higher Mind

- First get into a quiet space, Ground and be in the Center of Your Head.

- If you find noise and distraction anywhere in your space, take a few moments with the Rose tool or Grounding Cord to eliminate it.
- Anchor your attention in the Center of Your Head and be totally there. Notice the experience of the energy there. Is it clear? Quiet? Peaceful?
- When you are ready, move your attention up approximately one inch (2.5 cm) from the Center of Your Head.
- Then move your attention one and one-half inches (3.8 cm) toward the back of your head.
- Now return to the Center of Your Head and notice the difference.
- Repeat this movement two or three times to get a sense of the feeling and movement.
- Then move to the Higher Mind again and remain there.
- Breathe and notice the energy and qualities here. Notice how being in the Higher Mind is different than being in the Center of Your Head. It may be a subtle difference, but there *is* a difference.
- Without thinking, notice the quiet and stillness. Notice also that within the quietness there is a large openness. Allow this to unfold effortlessly for you.
- Take a few moments and slowly move back and forth between the Center of Your Head and the Higher Mind to better anchor the experience of being in each.
- Return to your Higher Mind and remain there.
- Take a breath and open your eyes.

Notice if you dropped out of your Higher Mind. Did you return to the Center of Your Head when you opened your eyes? Both locations have value and although entering the Higher Mind is not difficult, remaining there and mastering all that it offers is an eternal unfolding.

The URL and QR code below will take you to a meditation that will assist you in discovering the Still Point of your Higher Mind. Notice how you feel before listening and again afterward.

www.masteringalchemy.com/mabook-tool4-highermind

CHAPTER FOURTEEN

Tool # 5

The Octahedron—
The Diamond of Light
Surrounding You

As the waves of energy step up, greater levels of Light, wisdom, and knowledge become increasingly available to you. The more you can anchor and consistently hold the Light within you, the quicker you will awaken and fulfill your spiritual purpose. As you begin to vibrate within the fifth dimensional consciousness, while still surrounded by third dimensional energy, it is very important to recognize and live within your own Personal Power Field. In Chapter Two, we mentioned the importance of having a container in which to hold the water you wish to drink. This next tool rebuilds your aura into a strong and stable geometric field, so your personal power and energy can remain with you, instead of being weakened and lost among external places and people. Constructing this sacred field—the container—and living within it, will allow you to view and experience your internal life and the world around you from a much more calm, quiet, confident, and elegant perspective.

In sacred geometry, there are five forms known as Platonic solids, each of which holds unique characteristics. One of these is the Octahedron. It consists of one four-sided pyramid pointing up, with a second four-sided pyramid connected at the base that points down. This appears as a diamond with eight faces. The definition of a Platonic solid is that, within each unique form (tetrahedron, cube, icosahedron, dodecahedron, octahedron), all lines are of equal length, all angles are of the same degree, and each face within the form is the same size and shape. The geometry also fits into a sphere with all points touching the sphere.

Besides being a strong vessel to contain your energy and personal power, this geometric field is also an antenna—a transmitter and a receiver. The Octahedron attracts and receives frequencies of thought. It also transmits your thoughts, intentions and desires in a clearer, more directed way. If you can manage your antenna, you can manage what your antenna transmits and receives. Constructing the Octahedron around you creates a powerful energy field, which aligns with the information of the Shift and your own internal guidance system.

Constructing the Octahedron

You can again use the Rose tool for this exercise, however, using a simple dot as a marker will also work too.

- Take a moment now and find your space. Check your Grounding Cord and be sure you are in the Center of Your Head or your Higher Mind.
- Hold your arm out in front of you and again pretend you are holding a Rose between your fingertips. Your eyes can be open or closed.
- Be aware of the noisy third dimension on the other side of your Rose. Take a breath.

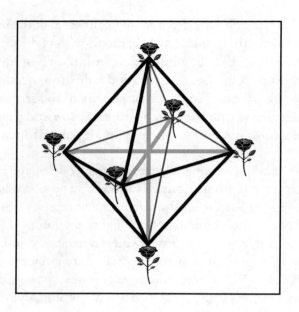

- Remember, this Rose operates in a circle surrounding you. Be aware of the 360 degrees and be aware of the Rose.
- Close your eyes. While being aware of the Rose in front of you, create a second Rose directly behind you on the circle. There is now one in front of you and one behind you. Feel them and/or 'see' them in your awareness.
- Now connect the two Roses by drawing an axis line that passes through your heart chakra, in the center of your chest.
- Hold those two Roses and the connecting line in place, while you create one more Rose on your right and another on your left.

TOOL # 5 - THE OCTAHEDRON

- Draw another axis line through your heart chakra connecting these two Roses. There are now four Roses, or dots, at equal distances around you.
- You need to establish two more points to set the Octahedron in place. Extend one arm straight up, above your head.
- Place a Rose, or dot, about 18 inches (46 cm) above your head.
- The final Rose is then placed about six inches (15 cm) below your feet, thus creating the six points of the Octahedron.
- Draw one more axis line, again passing through your heart chakra from the Rose, or dot, above you to the one below your feet.
- These axis lines passing through the heart create a gyroscope, which creates stabilization in your energy field.
- With your eyes closed, draw an imaginary line from the Rose in front of you to the one on your right. Really see it and feel it.
- Continue to draw the line to the Rose behind you, to the left of you, and then back to the Rose in front again. This completes the square at the level of your heart chakra.
- Next, trace four imaginary lines from the top Rose to the four Roses surrounding you, level with your heart chakra. You have now created a four-sided pyramid pointing up. Feel the change as if an umbrella surrounds you.
- Repeat the process from the point below you, up to each of the Roses surrounding you, creating the full Octahedron.

- Notice how you feel, surrounded by your Octahedron. The three axis lines help stabilize and keep you energetically balanced as you continue to build and activate your Personal Power Field.
- Bring your attention to the eight faces of your Octahedron, and fill these eight triangles with brilliant, translucent Light. Notice how this feels.

The space inside this geometry is yours, and only yours. Everything outside this field defines the rest of the universe. This diamond of Light that surrounds you now is not a wall or a defense system. It is a stable containment field that allows you to move around even more effectively, without becoming affected by external noise and drama. As an antenna, the Octahedron aligns with the universal, Infinite Intelligence being transmitted during this Shift. It creates an alignment with *all that you are*, and simply filters out *that which you are not*.

A long time ago this shape held the auric energy field in place, defining the boundaries of the physical vehicle for us. This was not for the purpose of separation, but rather to create a very clear definition of whom we each were, allowing for respect and clear communication. You have now rebuilt this sacred vessel around you.

The best way to reinforce this geometry and to own it for yourself is to trace the lines of the Octahedron repeatedly throughout your day and during your meditations. Make it fun and amusing. Reinforcing your Octahedron anchors it around you. If you consciously stay within your Light-filled Octahedron you will become less and less affected by other people's emotions, thoughts, and erratic behavior.

TOOL # 5 - THE OCTAHEDRON

What other people think of you, or how other people vibrate, is really none of your business. Your business is only about *you*. Your safety, your style, your joy, your enthusiasm, your passion, and your ability to express yourself, are all about you and your path. Interestingly, as you become more conscious within this geometry, your communication with others becomes more comfortable and enjoyable. Begin simply to regard everyone outside your Octahedron as actors in *your* play, performing for *your* entertainment. Play with this geometry as a new toy and make it fun. Construct it around you daily, reinforcing it whenever you feel the need. It won't take long to begin noticing the difference this tool makes in your day.

As you live and work within your Octahedron, you begin to align with the knowledge and the wisdom you once had. You also begin to transmit more clearly, and with greater strength, your intentions, desires and dreams for the Universe to see and reflect back to you. You begin to know yourself.

The URL and QR code below will take you to a meditation that walks you through building your Octahedron.

www.masteringalchemy.com/mabook-tool5-octahedron

CHAPTER FIFTEEN

Tool # 6
Activating Your Personal Power Field

As you built your sacred geometric field, the Octahedron, you may have noticed that the top portion is shorter than the lower portion. This is because it's not a fully completed Octahedron as yet. The following, final step will bring your field into a balanced geometric alignment. We will now build and activate your Personal Power Field. This is a self-contained, self-generated, spherical field of Light that completely surrounds the Octahedron and you.

We will begin with the third chakra, which is located in the solar plexus area within the physical body. To make it easy for you, below are simplified, step-by-step instructions, so you can practice this exercise for yourself. As with previous tools, if you find it easier or more comfortable to have someone guide you through this process, you can also listen to a special audio file on the Mastering Alchemy website that walks you through this important exercise. Details of how to access this appear at the end of this chapter.

- Find your space. Check your Octahedron and be in your Higher Mind.
- Notice the vertical axis line you created in the previous chapter, or recreate it here.

TOOL # 6 - ACTIVATING YOUR PERSONAL POWER FIELD

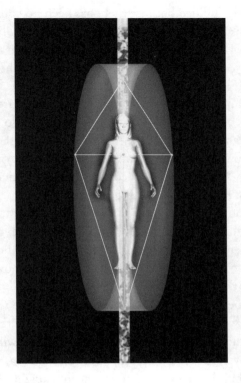

- Now create a line of Light that runs from the point of your Octahedron above you, through the center of your body, to the point of the Octahedron directly below you.
- Visualize another column of Light, approximately two inches in diameter, completely encircling that original line. This column also begins at the point above you and extends all the way to the point below you. In many instances, this column of Light is dormant; its purpose is

not being fulfilled because there has been no container to hold this flow of Light. However, now that you have built your Octahedron, you have a containment field that will enable you to begin to utilize this column for the purpose it was designed.

- We will now increase the speed at which the third chakra vibrates or spins by about twenty percent. To do this, sit quietly and be aware of the third chakra. Give the command to the third chakra to increase in speed by twenty percent. You may feel a speeding up, or excitement. You may not feel any change, and that's okay too.
- Next, move the energy up from the third chakra, through the column you just created and into the fourth chakra in the center of your sternum. Pause here and allow the energy to fill the chakra. You will intuitively know when the fourth chakra is filled with this Light.
- Continue moving the energy up the column to the fifth chakra, which resides in the soft portion of the throat.
- When the Light has filled your fifth chakra, it will then naturally continue on up into your sixth chakra, which is situated in the center of your forehead. Pause again.
- From there, the energy moves to the area at the top of your head, where the fontanelle resides in an infant. This is the seventh chakra.
- Once the energy in the central column reaches your seventh chakra, it begins to flow upward through the column to the point at the top of the Octahedron. Observe as it does this automatically. There is no need to push it.
- This energy then flows outward in all directions like a fountain of water. It flows down and around the outside

of your energy field, creating a sphere around you. It flows to the bottom of the column, where it is then drawn back up through the same, central column.
- This energy continues this pattern of flowing up, and around and down. It also begins to accelerate in speed.
- Once again, place your attention on your third chakra and give it the command to increase its energy flow by another twenty percent. As the energy increases, the energy distribution throughout your body also increases. Allow the energy to move up through the central column, and as it enters the fourth chakra again, notice that the energy begins to spin in that chakra as well.
- Remember to keep your breathing flowing rhythmically in a smooth, circular, uninterrupted motion.
- The spinning increases and continues its pattern, moving up through the fifth and sixth chakras, and finally surging into and out of the top of the seventh chakra as it continues upward.
- As the energy pushes upwards and out, it flows like a waterfall all around your field, covering 360 degrees of the egg-shaped field that surrounds the Octahedron. As it flows down and around, the energy is magnetically pulled back into the bottom of the column and up through it again.
- At this point you might feel a little pulsing sensation or a bit of pressure. You may become aware of your heartbeat, or have a sense that something is beginning to pull upwards inside of you. It's also fine if you don't experience this, some of us don't. Just know that this is occurring.
- The energy continues to move in a circular flow. It moves

in, through, and around your body, through the central column, out and around your energy field, and back into the bottom of the column again.

- As this flow of your energy continues, you will now issue four commands, each of which will double the speed of the energy. You may become aware of a sensation of energy beginning to rise as you accelerate your field. You may not notice anything different. Either response is correct. Just allow it to occur. Be amused, curious, and very pleased with yourself.
- Now, fasten your seatbelt, and for the first time, mentally command the field to double in speed. Allow the energy to accelerate upwards until you feel a little pressure at the top of your head. For some people, the energy has a tendency to pull them up out of their body, so remember to stay anchored in the Center of Your Head or your Higher Mind. Pretend to see out of your closed eyes if that helps.
- As the energy continues to pick up speed, give a second command for it to again double in speed. Notice what is occurring as you allow it to accelerate, and the energy begins to move faster inside the column.
- Next, command the column to expand from two inches to eight inches (20 cm) in diameter. Watch as the flow slows a bit as it has more room to move. This will cause the energy inside your body to relax and make room for the third doubling.
- Command the speed to double for the third time, and as you feel the energy moving faster and higher, allow yourself and your body to relax. If you notice a little pressure in your eyes, or on the top of your head, relax,

TOOL # 6 - ACTIVATING YOUR PERSONAL POWER FIELD

and simply allow it to be a validation that something is going on. You are changing yourself. There's nothing to think about. Your body and your Higher Self know exactly what to do. You are simply rewiring, rebuilding, and remembering yourself.

- Now, before you give the command to double for the fourth and final time, just take a few moments to allow the field to slow down a little. Allow it to seek its own balance and to stabilize. The axis lines that you put in place earlier will assist with this. Don't worry; the energy will not turn off. Once it's turned on it will stay on.

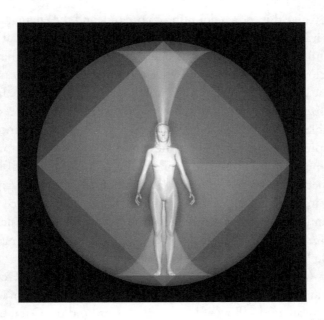

- We are now going to expand the energy flow for the fourth time, and something very specific is going to happen. In addition to the energy continuing up and fountaining out at the top of the energy field in a consistent linear flow, the energy will now begin to spin in the column. As it begins to flow up the column, it will spin in a clockwise manner (from your left around to the front-right of you). As it spins clockwise, it begins to both compress and accelerate at an increased rate. You won't feel any pressure or exaggeration because the acceleration is very smoothly orchestrated within the column.

As you give this fourth doubling command, and the energy begins to spiral out at the top, it also begins to put the spherical field around you into motion. The energy will spiral around the field in a clockwise manner, and then accelerate even more as it moves up the column. As it does this, it will reach a point where it will stabilize at a very high, fast speed and then settle into a nice, comfortable sensation. Another thing you may notice as you increase the spin of this energy is that the shape of your Octahedron has become more balanced and aligned. The spin of the field of Light will become perfectly spherical, and the Octahedron will expand outward so that each of the six points will be equal distance from each other; all touching the edge of the sphere. There is no need to analyze this, just experience and enjoy it. The higher, wiser aspect of you knows exactly what it is doing.

Now, without opening your eyes, become aware of the Octahedron and sphere you have created. Notice how it feels. From inside it, be aware of this flow of Light spinning around the Octahedron and accelerating back up through the column within you. At this point you may be feeling less pressure, cooler, more stabilized, and more comfortable.

Congratulations!

This is where it begins to get really interesting. You've successfully built a new energy field from which to create your life. The more you play with this, the more you will develop a new awareness of yourself, and of the fact that there is something different about how you now move around.

Spinning the Octahedron and More
A story from Jim

An interesting thing about this particular piece of work that you just did is that when I first began teaching this, the Archangels didn't tell me everything. They simply told me to try it and see what happened. So a group of about twenty students and I followed their instructions and began doubling the speed of the energy as you just did. Initially, we could only maintain this speed for about thirty seconds. We would then have to stop, and everyone would fall on the floor for about thirty minutes in a daze, exclaiming, "Whoa! That was really amazing." This continued for about five weeks, with all of us repeating this scenario each week. It was very fascinating for all of us.

After five weeks, the Archangels said, "Well, that was great. Now follow these additional instructions and take the field to ten percent the speed of Light."

"No problem." We said. We all followed the new instructions and went up to ten percent. Once again, we could only hold it for about thirty seconds before everyone would need to lie on the floor for another thirty minutes. It was hysterical.

This continued for several more weeks until we began to get smart and realized that there was much more the Archangels had in store for us. With a few additional, very specific, directions we eventually took the field to ninety percent the speed of Light. Everyone was on the floor… and there was no going back. There were no more instructions for a while, so we continued to practice each week and we soon acclimated to the new, higher energies.

Then the Archangels revealed, "Together, you are anchoring something that has been lost and unavailable on the Earth and to humanity for a very long time." This small group of twenty-one in a small town in Northern California anchored something very, very powerful.

Eventually we began to offer this work around the country and around the world. More and more people did what you just did, and more. It took less and less time, and less falling on the floor. Now, when I do this with participants in our Level 1 program, we are able to accomplish a great deal in just a few minutes. It's quite humorous because people look at me now and say, "What's the big deal?" The big deal is *you don't know it's a big deal*. Such a great amount has been anchored from the thousands of people before you, that you can simply step onto the path they created and follow in their footsteps. It is now easier and quicker for you. It is as if there was a big wall of ice. People would chip and chip away at it, and they would have their experience with this work. The next weekend, the group right behind them would walk up and begin exactly where the previous group had left off. They would chip away for a short while, and have their experience with the work while preparing the path for the group following behind them.

And now here you are, following the many, many footsteps before you, adding to All That Is. As we continue through the remainder of this book, it is your turn to add to All That Is and make the path a little easier for the person standing close behind you. So, right now, enjoy the journey, enjoy the pathway, and enjoy the fourth dimension. And let's see what living in a sacred, geometric field of Light feels like. Be happy; take a breath.

Scan the QR code below, or type the URL in your browser to access an audio file containing a meditation that will guide you through this exercise. Sit back in the chair and let's see what exciting new experiences you can create.

www.masteringalchemy.com/mabook-tool6-powerfield

CHAPTER SIXTEEN

Tool # 7
The Living Words

There is a statement in an old book somewhere that says, "In the beginning was the Word." Words are very valuable in our life, and we use them in many, many ways, but we will now begin to experience words within a new and different relationship. The Law of Attraction understands vibrations. So in the beginning there was the word, but actually, in the beginning there was the *vibration,* or the *configuration of vibrations,* that created a reality.

We have discussed the fact that many people walk around experiencing what they don't want to experience—words like depression, anger, or frustration. Again, the Law of Attraction, which is flawless, will recognize that word and vibration and give you all things like it. You also know that when you hold those vibrations in the lower frequencies it is really very difficult to create positive experiences for yourself. When you are depressed, or frustrated, or feeling resentful, it is difficult, or impossible, to create and attract positive, fun experiences. The energy, or if you can imagine, the molecules of your life, compress and tighten down, creating no room or space for you to move around freely.

Conversely, you have had times when you were happy, exhilarated, and enthusiastic. In those particular moments, it is as if the molecules get further apart, and the opportunity to create seems to be much easier. You are no longer trying to navigate through the rigidness, but instead, have the freedom that those faster vibrations offer. Creating and moving through your experiences is much less restricted in these higher and faster vibrations.

Let's take a look at words, not so much as *words*, but as *vibrations*. We will begin to structure and experience these vibrations as emotions and feelings. This will begin to create a platform that allows you to create and experience your life on your terms, within your own chosen vibrations and words.

Choosing Happy

Have you ever noticed how often people say, "I am _____ (something)…?"

"I am sick."
"I am uncomfortable."
"I am struggling and swamped."
"I am worn out."
"I am having a really difficult day"

Statements such as these generate energy in a very strong way. They act like a magnet, so that whatever follows the words "I am…" is attracted to you with greater speed and fullness. Hence, it's important to be mindful of what you say, and how you say it. If you can begin to create a distinction between the problem ("I am sick") and yourself, you will find that things can occur around you and you don't have to identify with them, or take them on and become them. You can choose to radiate or say,

"I am fine… and my nose is stuffed up today."
"I am surrounded with problems and I am doing okay."

> "Even though I am in the midst of all my stuff today, I am kind of fascinated by it."

The concept of choosing your feelings may sound odd. Feelings are feelings, right? They just happen to us. No, they don't *just happen* to us. The fact is, we can *choose* how we experience our thoughts and emotions. We are not victims to the energy that moves through us. Our emotions are simply charged energy in motion, and as you have discovered and experienced in previous chapters, you are very capable and able to shift and manage energy. Sure, feelings or emotions happen instantly and unconsciously at first, like a wave that rushes through the body... until you decide to increase your awareness and be the creator of your life, rather than accepting what is on the doorstep when you awake in the morning.

Choosing does not mean suppressing or denying how you really feel. Grief, anger, sadness, and fear are all real experiences. Observing the feeling, acknowledging it, and then choosing something new is key. Ignoring emotions, or slapping a bandage on them, may keep them submerged in the unconsciousness where they could fester, keep you stuck, alter your perceptions, and make you sick.

Here is a short exercise that will help you experience the vibration and feelings that words possess and how they demonstrate themselves in your space:

- Be in the Center of Your Head, take a breath and then close your eyes. Take as much time as necessary to find your space.
- Remember a time in your past when you had a Happy experience. (If 'Happy' is too difficult to grab, try an easier word—perhaps satisfied or content.)

- Take a moment and put yourself clearly in that past Happy moment. See the flower, or the child laughing… hear the joke that somebody made… accept the compliment that someone gave you. Allow yourself to be fully in that experience. Remember the memory, feel the feeling. Be that word, Happy. Take your time. Get happiness all over you. Roll around in it. Really *feel* it, hear it, and taste it fully.
- As you allow yourself to completely be this energy vibration, notice how much bigger the smile on your face gets. Laughing is acceptable here. *Fee-e-e-l* the happiness in your body.
- Return your attention to remembering that experience and feel the feeling all over again. Notice what you notice. Where does that feeling live in your body? What color is it? Does it have a shape? Just make it up. Pretend to be Happy. *Fee-e-e-l* it in your body. And breathe.
- Feel the feeling, and now allow the thought and memory of the original experience to fade from your awareness while you continue to feel the feeling in your body. Notice that the happiness you are feeling right now is a *present time* feeling. It's not in the *past time* feeling and memory.
- Feelings are experienced in the present moment and can ONLY be experienced in the present moment. Although you were recalling a memory experienced in a past moment that included the feeling of Happy, Happy as a feeling (or any other feeling you place your attention upon) can only be experienced in a *present time* moment.

Let's do this again with another word.

- Shift your attention and find the feeling of being Certain. Notice how Certain stimulates a different kind of feeling than Happy. In simple terms, you know how to turn the key in the ignition of your car, right? Can you make your car's engine start? Are you sure? Do you know it in terms of an awareness, a feeling of Certainty? "YES… Every time I turn the key in the ignition I start the car." I AM Certain.
- Good. Now simply feel this feeling of Certain. Take your time and really recognize this energy. *Be* the feeling.
- You may find that your body needs to move a bit and adjust to this new energy. If you feel the need to sit up in your chair, straighten your shoulders, raise your head, or extend your chest a little, and do so. Then take a breath, and right now feel Certain.
- Where does the vibration of Certain, or Certainty, live in your body? What color is it? Does it have a shape? Just make it up. Pretend to be Certain. *Fee-e-e-l* it in your body. Recognize it. Own the feeling of being Certain. This feeling is yours. Know that nobody can take this away from you. It is always there for you to choose and access. Most of the time we forget this and shift our attention away from *who we are* to other vibrations.
- As you are being Certain, without making any movement, also be Happy. Allow yourself to smile. Go ahead; give yourself permission. Nobody can take this away from you, and nobody ever has taken it away

from any of us. All we have done is allow others to overshadow *who we really are*, and then we've moved to experience those less comfortable vibrations.

As you begin to play with and really 'get' Happy and Certain, which are just two of many vibrations, you begin to have an opportunity to accelerate your path. These words are the vibrations and feelings that naturally define *who you are* and *have always been*. These words are the vibrations that you have turned away from in order to play the game of the third dimension. Identifying and BEING the vibrations of Certain and Happy (try Capable and Present also) are the beginning of your ascension. You are creating a platform that will allow you to observe the third dimension as it simply dissolves and reshapes itself into the fifth dimension.

Integrating these Living Words begins to create a platform from which to manage your life. Additional Living Words you will want to weave into this platform include Capable (as in Powerful), Commanding, Present, Senior or Seniority (as in owning your Self, this is who I AM) and Gracious. These seven words are not random. They have been specifically chosen to assist us in the Shift, to accelerate a path that we are remembering.

As you begin to play with these seven specific Living Words, you will find yourself much more able to manage your attention and to observe all that is going on around you without being distracted and pulled away from your center. You will discover that every experience you have will be quite different from your previous experiences. Instead of being knocked out of your space by things that are outside of you, you can simply choose to allow all insults, distractions, or noise to pass you by. All you have to do is find the word, or group of words, that would most effortlessly uplift the situation that you are encountering—e.g., *What platform of words do I want to wear or vibrate at when I step into this meeting? What three vibrations do I want to present myself in today? What single word would I like to replace this ugly feeling with?* Begin simply. Don't choose words such as Love or Peace. Those are too complicated, and too far away from where you might be vibrating right now. The key is to make this real, simple, and very easy to grasp.

Here is an exercise that will help interrupt your third dimensional habits and help you move more rapidly down this path:

- First, create a list of words. Choose words that make you feel good. Select words that you would like to be known by in your world. For example, insightful, kind, respectful, purposeful, gracious, grateful, honest, dignified, caring, or helpful. Make it a long list, choosing words that will help you remember your Self. Doing so will assist you in consciously and deliberately creating choices.
- Next, choose seven of those words that make you feel especially good. Choose words that you aspire to experience, or would like to *be*.

Take one of these seven words each day for a week and *be* that word. Demonstrate this word in every situation and notice how it makes you feel. You will notice that when you become intentional about being the word, you feel more alert and aware, more present in the *now moment*. You will feel and be in charge of yourself on your own terms. If you find you have slipped out of the word, simply smile and become the word once again.

When you begin to hold a vibration as a word, you begin to anchor that energy in your daily reality. As you *become* these various words and try them on as coats, you will discover that you can now consciously choose how to create and manage your life rather than simply accepting the defaults that you have allowed others to impose upon you. *I am not okay, I don't deserve, I will never be good enough, I'm stupid* will fade from your reality.

Another interesting thing happens when you begin to wear the Living Words, and the other words on your list; your physical body, emotional body, and mental body all begin to follow suit. As you begin to raise your vibration in this manner, the Law of Attraction responds by feeding you even more of what you are wearing and feeling (Happy, Certain, Gracious, etc.). All aspects of your life move into well-being—physically, emotionally and mentally.

The Living Words that we are playing with—Happy, Certain, Senior, Present, Capable (Powerful), Gracious, and Commanding—are not arbitrary words. They are not just randomly selected. They are very specific, and they open some amazing doors for you. If you can begin to weave these words into the fabric of the coats that you wear, you will discover new and fascinating things begin to happen. Simply by holding these vibrations you will begin to attract people, situations and opportunities to you in a very different manner than you have in the past.

Creating your own set of Living Words, and learning to *feel* them, rather than think them, is one of the most important things you can do during this incredible time of Shift. Standing upon this vibrational platform, and adjusting it according to whatever situation lies before you, will enable you to create the reality that you desire. This is not complicated; it simply is a reconfiguration from the third dimensional way of life to a higher, clearer way of being. It can become a conscious moment-to-moment choice. This is a way of life that is Happy, Present, Certain, Senior, Powerful, Commanding and Gracious.

Your life becomes a life you choose and direct.

There is a great deal more to the Living Words than we have covered here. In addition to having the power to rewire you, words have color, vibrational tone, and the ability to activate aspects of your Light Body. In Chapter Twenty Six we will discuss these other aspects of words and how they are a huge stepping stone on the pathway to ascension.

Scan the QR code below or type the URL into your browser to access a page that contains a meditation to help you anchor this information about the Living Words.

www.masteringalchemy.com/mabook-tool7-livingwords

CHAPTER SEVENTEEN

Using The Tools to Make Your Job More Fun

Business meetings, in fact any group meetings, can often be uncomfortable and laborious. Here's how you can use a combination of tools to help a meeting, event, or new encounter become more enjoyable and fun.

A meeting is a group of individuals with unique thoughts and beliefs coming together to find common agreements. Sometimes they meet to discover the thoughts and beliefs they share and establish the company or group culture. Each of them wants to move forward into success. Perhaps they meet to decide the direction of the corporation, how to market a new product, or simply when the company party will be held. Everyone attending has his or her own agenda, and list of dislikes and must-haves, as well as their own expectations of how the meeting will proceed (based upon past experience of such gatherings).

How to make meetings successful for *you*

So how do you, as a leader or participant, armed with energy tools, hold a meeting that is fun, task-oriented, short, and successful? There are plenty of manuals out there that tell you how to run a productive business meeting. This may be the first one that suggests ways to pre-pave the way for one from a non-physical perspective. What is about to be explained can be applied to any situation that you know will soon be arriving in your life. It could be a date, a conversation with your son, a shopping trip, a vacation, a test, a new art project or a dinner party. The same tools and techniques apply to any upcoming event. We'll use the situation of a business meeting to illustrate the combining of tools here.

Whether you are leading the meeting or are a participant, this meeting is *for* you. It has entered your life at this moment to offer you something. It may be here for you to be amused and entertained. It may be here for you to learn something new. It may be in your life to give you the opportunity to hold your boundaries and maintain your balance—no matter what happens during the meeting. Only from a foundation of balance can you make the meeting work for you. Remember the meetings you've attended where an attendee (or even the leader) lost his balance and became affected by the others around him? Perhaps the company bully challenged him, or the boss asked a question he hadn't prepared for. Remember how he stumbled painfully and perhaps never really regained his balance? When you combine a few of these tools to pave the way prior to the meeting, you can ensure the desired results unfold in an extremely amusing and stress-free way. You also allow the other attendees to have a great time and reach their goals simultaneously. It's win-win for everyone.

To begin, choose a simple event that will occur within the next week or two. Choose something that is relatively easy already—an event that you may feel some anticipation toward, but not a tremendous amount of anxiety about. A day or two prior to the meeting set aside an hour when you can sit quietly where you won't be disturbed. This won't work if you are charged or negative in any way, so play with it with an uncharged, neutral attitude. If you find yourself becoming charged, judgmental or off-balance, simply take a moment, breathe, check your field, your tools and return to a place of neutrality. Watch the movie unfold before you.

- Find your space.
- From the Center of Your Head, or Higher Mind, imagine a giant Rose in the center of the empty meeting room. This will still work, even if you don't know what the room looks like. Make it up.
- Give the Rose a glow of whichever color represents the energy you'd personally like to experience in this room and during this meeting. Make it up. Red or black are not light, comfortable choices.
- Attach Grounding Cords to all corners of the meeting room and command them to release any energy that might already be in the room that won't support success.
- Begin to add aspects and words to the Rose in the center of the room; aspects that you'd like to experience during the meeting. Possibilities include: permission, amusement, equality, efficient, abundance, patience, success, honesty, warmth, focus, camaraderie, plenty of time, cooperation, happy, good jokes, and ease.
- Create a new Rose at the entry door. This serves as a decompression Rose, assisting all who walk through it to relax, leave the rest of the world behind them, and continue in *present time*.
- Imagine each of the attendees entering the room. As they enter say, 'Hello' and take a moment to welcome each one personally. Invite them to have a seat. This works even if you are not familiar with the appearance of the attendees.

- Put a Grounding Cord on each sitting attendee, and command the Cord to release from their space any electrical and magnetic energies that keep their attention out of *present time* and prevent them from matching the words you put into the Rose sitting in the center of the room. It is not necessary to get into the specific energies here.
- Now imagine you are sitting in the meeting room. Ground yourself, and see yourself smiling within your Octahedron.
- Visualize the sphere that surrounds you at a color that represents Certainty to you. Imagine the word Certainty written somewhere on it. If another word is more appropriate, substitute that one.
- Alternatively, you could imagine yourself standing firmly on a platform of a few words that you would like to experience at the meeting—e.g., Certainty, Calm, Graceful. Cooperation, etc.
- Now visualize the meeting in progress. Just make it up. Imagine everyone enthusiastic, creative and participatory. Imagine only the best. Don't get stuck on making it perfect or realistic.
- If you notice any negative thoughts coming up as you play, simply Ground them, or collect them in a Rose and blow them up.
- When you feel complete, or the imaginary meeting comes to a conclusion, visualize everyone leaving the meeting room in high spirits, successful, and enthusiastic.
- Re-Ground the meeting room to drain away any additional disruptive words, emotions, and energy.

- Remember a time when you felt Successful and Grateful. Feel those feelings now.
- Your preparation is complete. You may check your space and your Octahedron. Like yourself and continue with your day.

You may do this portion of the pre-paving several times prior to the event, changing and adding details as you wish.

On the day of the meeting

- Find your quiet space again, and be in the Center of Your Head, at neutral.
- Recreate the giant Rose in the center of the room and imagine the meeting in progress.
- Give the Rose a glow of a color that represents the energy you'd like to experience today.
- Re-Ground the room.
- Look around the imaginary meeting room and notice what you notice.
- Ground yourself, and reset the platform with a few words that fit today.
- When all is as you like it, feel Gratitude and let the image fade away.
- Remember a time when you felt Successful. Feel that now.
- Fill up your space and *be* the Living Words and energy you just created.
- Step into the meeting with your Grounding Cord attached, your platform at Certainty and Success, and your Octahedron in place or your Rose in front of you.

- Like yourself.
- Smile.
- Be pleased wth yourself.

CHAPTER EIGHTEEN

Tool # 8
The Strength of Silence

As this amazing Shift of Consciousness continues to unfold in and around us, the noise and drama is becoming louder and more distracting. Be aware of the world now and compare it to what was happening a few years ago. The noise and drama is indeed increasing and intensifying. But you don't have to be affected by it. Silence is your power and strength. It is both the tool and the sanctuary that will keep you sane and intact.

Recently on NPR there was an interview with a scientist who studies the effects of technology on humans. He observed that many people who are continually using electronic communication devices are losing their ability to be quiet and alone. They are texting, Skyping, calling, and Facebooking so much that when the device is not demanding their attention, the adults and kids quickly experience the absence of dialogue as loneliness. Their reaction then is immediately to initiate new exchanges to fill the quiet. They have forgotten how to appreciate their alone time and the value of quietness. Learning this skill and having the ability to remain silent would enhance their well-being.

Have you ever been in a conversation where the person you are talking to doesn't stop talking long enough for you to contribute? Or perhaps you've received emails from someone who isn't filtering their words and includes so much irrelevant information it is difficult to understand their point? How does that energy feel in your space?

Imagine being in a conversation with a noisy person with your Rose up, observing from your Higher Mind, or the Center of Your Head. You sit before them with a quiet, centered, detached demeanor, yet very alert. Observing and waiting can be a very powerful response to their noise. Not reacting when someone is throwing energy or demonstrating other charged emotions is not only empowering for you, it can be a huge empowerment for them too. By this, I mean that you are not offering them resistance nor anything to argue with. You are not adding fuel to their fire. You are simply demonstrating another way of being. Very shortly they will have worked themselves up, through, and then over their intensity without getting it all over you. Or, they won't, and instead they'll move on to someone else who may or may not choose to wallow around in the mud with them.

Have you ever been in a meeting where the 'perceived leader' is really not the 'true leader'? The true leader is the quiet one. She is the one who silently and patiently waits and watches, stays in her space, and knows exactly when and how to respond. Most often the true leader is not the one who does most of the talking.

We are all being asked to step up and become the leaders and teachers we came here to be. To do this, we must learn to walk through the noise and drama of the third dimension, while holding the higher aspects of the fourth and fifth dimensions. Once we master this quiet observation, we can respond from the platform of Wisdom, Grace, and Compassion, instead of shoot-ready-aim from a place of reaction.

It is of critical importance for each of us to be aware of where we have our attention, and how we are moving through this important time of Shift. To be a citizen of the fifth dimension, we each will learn to be the master of our every thought, every emotion, every word, and every action, in every moment. Sound impossible? It is not. However, some assembly is required.

Silence offers a number of advantages:

- It provides the opportunity to observe, choose, and then act
- It allows you to observe and respond to a situation in the present moment, as it is unfolding, rather than reacting from habit or bias
- It allows you to choose the appropriate action before you act
- It allows you to observe and evaluate the results of your chosen action, and then adjust your next possible action as the situation unfolds
- And most importantly, silence allows you be involved in the situation, with the intention of bringing about a positive result for all involved.

Ask yourself these questions before responding to any situation:

- Will my next comment or action add value to this? Is what I'm about to do or say absolutely necessary?
- Is it possible my response might create an imbalance, wobble, or big mess that I, or someone else, will have to clean up later?
- Will my next comment or action add anything to make a difference, or am I adding to the noisiness?
- Can this thing I'm about to say or do wait?

- Is this situation even my problem? In other words, is this situation someone else's concern and I am simply meddling in something that is not my issue?

If you can slow down and take a moment to ask yourself these questions, you will discover that many of what you may think are responses, are, instead, 3D reactions. They are a result of unconscious habit, much of which adds no value or assistance.

A reminder about these tools

The tools you have just played with in this section are simple, but make no mistake; they will change your life. Once you practice and anchor these tools into your day, they become a way of life like no other. Experience and play with all of the energy tools in this section often. As simple as they are, they will alter your conscious reality, and allow you to enjoy the unfolding Shift.

CHAPTER NINETEEN

Where Do All These Tools Lead?

There is much more beyond the tools we have offered here. The next section will explore in greater depth a few of the tools and concepts we have discussed and offer new ones. As you use these simple, practical tools, your life will change in some quite wonderful ways. Please see the section entitled 'Success Stories' for some examples of what is possible for you.

This is what we have observed in ourselves and in others

- The ability to clear energy in the body to such an extent to promote healing and greater well-being
- Creating and receiving the preferred outcome of a circumstance
- Greater communication and understanding of the inner guidance system, its messages and directions
- The end to worry and stress
- Have the certainty and power to step into new situations with confidence and success
- Attract new friends, co-creators and partners who are more aligned with the life you wish to experience
- The ability to make far better choices and decisions that benefit you and others

- Having time and resources quickly available to achieve goals
- Knowing what works for you and what doesn't.

The personal experiences that are now available to you

The Sanctuary of the Pink Diamond

There is a special room within your heart center, the Sacred Heart, called the Sanctuary of the Pink Diamond. Much happens here. This is where you meet and begin to merge with your Soul, to know all that the Soul knows. You and other aspects or Extensions of your Soul will come together in this Sanctuary to anchor all they know and have experienced about feminine and masculine wisdom and creativity. In this special room, you will meet Rose of Light, an ascended Being who will gift you with something very wonderful. From here, you will journey to the center of the Earth to expand your connection with Gaia.

The Three Kingdoms

There is a wonderful experience now available to you where you meet representatives of the Animal, Angelic and Mineral Kingdoms, who invite you into their worlds. Here, you heal the wounds that occurred during your lifetimes in Atlantis and together, expand harmony between those Kingdoms and humanity.

Journeys to the temples

Within the fifth dimension, there are temples you can and will visit—the Temple of Purification and the Temple of Flame, to name two.

Other geometries

Like the Octahedron, the other Platonic solids and other geometries are antennas that send and receive unique information, activations and energies. You can transform the Octahedron into the Star Tetrahedron. You can also work with the Tetrahedron to clear the veils of ignorance and forgetfulness, and the Cube to create environments much like the 'holodeck' on Star Trek.

Flying

Remember those flying dreams you used to have as a kid? Well, they were very real, and it is possible to direct them consciously now. The Orange Dragonfly will assist you.

The Rays of Creation

These are the building blocks of all creations. They are the creative tools and steps to create everything. They are used to deconstruct old reference points and experiences, and construct new ones, as well as to rearrange the fabric and structure of the life you have known into what you came here to experience.

These are just a small sample of what awaits you as you begin to practice and integrate the tools and skills that are available. They offer a new way of life that is far grander than anything you can imagine.

The QR code and URL on the following page will take you to a page containing one of our most popular meditations, the Three Kingdoms, which offers one of many profound experiences that are now available to you.

WHAT DO YOU MEAN THE THIRD DIMENSION IS GOING AWAY?

www.masteringalchemy.com/mabook-ch19-threekingdoms

SECTION III

Advancing Your Skills

CHAPTER TWENTY

You Are Rewiring Yourself

Just as with the Mastering Alchemy Programs, the goal of this book is about *you* creating *yourself*. It is about remembering, rewiring, becoming, and being. It is about you clearing the veils of forgetfulness and putting yourself back together. It is not about thinking or intellectualizing. This is not like reading a book about birdhouses and then thinking and figuring out how to use the material in it. It is about actively engaging with, feeling, and experiencing the creative mechanism that is this work.

Although you may be unconscious of it, you haven't just been 'reading' this book, or 'playing' with the information we are sharing. You are also playing on the etheric levels during those hours when you sleep. You see, this work and play doesn't end when you lay down this book. The changes you are making continue as you sleep. When you make the personal commitment to remember yourself, every aspect of you enthusiastically joins in the party. Mental, emotional, physical and non-physical changes take place. As you sleep, you are still very conscious on the etheric levels. Each night as you go Home, you return to the full, higher, multi-dimensional consciousness *that you are*, and you begin to work in a way that allows you, in the physical, to remember and to recreate yourself quickly, fully, and efficiently.

One of the many things that occur as you practice these tools and integrate this information is that you begin to combine and merge your mental and emotional bodies. You merge your thoughts and emotions, and a new reality begins to form. This is not difficult to do, but it does require that you skillfully align the aspects of your *in*tention and manage your *at*tention point in the process. It is impossible to create this greater level of consciousness from the third dimensional *past-future time* structure. It requires you to be in *present time*, fully aware and focused.

Moving from being unconscious to being aware

Another outcome of integrating these tools and rewiring yourself is that you shift from *reacting to* your third dimensional environment to *intentionally creating* your fourth and fifth dimensional reality. This occurs as you deliberately move out of the third dimensional unconsciousness and into higher fourth and fifth dimensional awareness. It unfolds like this:

- First you realize that you are, or have been, unconscious of being unconscious. (Most of humanity is unconscious of being unconscious as they walk around in the third dimension.)
- Then you become conscious of being unconscious; you recognize your unconscious habits and thoughts, and begin to eliminate them.
- This moves you to become conscious of being conscious; you begin to notice that you are rarely out of *present time* awareness, and hence are rarely affected by the noise and drama that may surround you. This step can occur quickly.
- You then become aware of being aware. It is at this moment that you are in partnership with your Soul, knowing

more of what your Soul knows, and acting and choosing as your Soul would.

This process of awakening requires a deliberate *in*tention to know yourself, as well as purposefully holding your *at*tention on that intention. If you have been practicing the exercises and participating in the online meditations and lectures provided, you are definitely in the process of both recognizing the noise, and resetting yourself (through your antenna, the Octahedron) to raise your vibration above the noise and drama. You are successfully beginning to reshape, rewire, and realign yourself with your own truths and with *who you really are*. You are on your way to becoming aware of being aware.

What can make the rewiring happen faster?

It is important to remember that much more occurs in the *non-doing*, in other words, by simply *being*, than in the thinking and working. It is in the allowing that all the energy flows into the Heart. The rewiring begins to occur in the field of awareness outside of the rational mind's ability to understand what is happening.

So—here again, as tempting as it is to hurry, you will accomplish more in a much shorter period of time if you can temper your impulse to hurry and have no *need* to figure it out. Be comfortable sitting with the information you are receiving without knowing what to do with it. Just allow the experience to flow through you. This isn't a race. Remember, the slower you go, the faster you will arrive.

CHAPTER TWENTY ONE

You Are Not Your Problem

Have you ever set out in a great mood to meet a friend at a café for coffee, only to spend a miserable hour or two listening to how rotten their finances/relationship/job is? Suddenly, the delightful day you had been anticipating dissolved into something far less enjoyable, and no matter what you did to shift your attention and raise your spirits, you never quite managed to get your energy back to the same level as when you started your day. We have all experienced this dynamic in our life, but we rarely understand or pay attention to what occurred. What happens in situations like this is that we unconsciously match that other person's energy and then let it affect our entire day.

Now consider the following interchange. The six mangers at a juice factory meet monthly to update each other on production, customer service, sales, etc. The meetings have always been short, productive, and fun. Today, Sam, who works in shipping, has had a frustrating day with no-show employees, broken machines, and customer complaints. When it was his turn to update everyone, he stood up, revved up his energy, and began loudly complaining about how bad things are, how no other department is doing their job, and how no one is getting paid enough. "Ain't it Awful!" Sam was throwing his opinions and energy out to the group, and within minutes, some of the participants were loudly agreeing with his complaints. What began as a productive meeting quickly escalated into a gripe session interspersed with thick, uncomfortable silences. What happened was that the participants were unconsciously matching Sam's strong, charged energy, which moved them from personal balance to imbalance. The result was no one had a good time; the meeting lasted twice as long as usual, and very little was accomplished.

Developing the skill of discernment

Here lies a great opportunity to assist your friend at the café, enhance the meeting, and become more masterful yourself. The energy of the problem the person is focusing upon, and the energy of the person, are two decidedly distinct things. The problem and the person are not the same. As you discern and become the observer of the situation, you are able to choose how you wish to engage. You may not necessarily agree with the energy of the problem, but you won't automatically jump in to fix it. You listen from behind your Rose, within your Octahedron, and hold a tone that feels good to you—Happy, Kind, Aware—and a sense of your own well-being.

Understanding the mechanics of these interchanges can be extremely useful. In the past, before you had these tools, you might have matched the energy of others in order to understand their problem or situation. As in the examples above, once you match that energy, you may physically/emotionally feel the sticky, heavy discomfort of the problem the other person is holding. However, there is another choice. As you become more conscious and masterful, the valuable skill of Discerning becomes available to you. Instead of matching that loud, chaotic energy, engaging with it, and getting it all over you, you can simply observe it, discern if it is your problem, and then choose how, or if, you want to get involved.

You might say, "Gosh, I hear what you are saying about this mess you are in, but before we go there, how was your son's graduation yesterday?" In this case you are helping them separate their energy and attention that is *in* the problem *from* the problem itself. You are discerning the difference between the person and their problem. Your friend and the problem are never the same unless they match and become one with the problem. As you change the focus and begin to create room to view the problem in a very different, less engaged manner, your friend will too. Soon, the charged issue they had a moment ago is not as important or hopeless. You, and they, begin to discern the difference between *being the problem* and *observing the problem*.

We all live our problems far too often. How often have you, like your friend, complained that you don't have enough money, you're sick, depressed, tired, sad, or otherwise not okay? The truth is you have never been *not okay*. It is impossible to be *not okay*. Most, however, have never even considered this concept. You can have a cold, feel depressed, and have money problems, but you are always okay. When you begin to discern and recognize the difference between I am okay and I happen to have a problem with money, feeling sad, or sick, then you have the power to change and rearrange your circumstances. When you identify with and match the problem, rev it up, worry about it, and let it run through your body, you and the problem are in the same uncomfortable space. You can never solve the problem while in the midst of it. You have no power to adjust your circumstance when you are revved up, engulfed in, and overwhelmed by it. Once you understand that you cannot be *not okay*, you are no longer a victim to the situation.

From this new awareness, your problem becomes a circumstance, and you now have the necessary room to consider new and different potential solutions. You are okay, AND you are surrounded by a mess. You are not the mess.

When you find yourself in a high intensity drama, it is time to congratulate yourself, not beat yourself up. Most people go about their lives never noticing how their noise and drama affect themselves, their environment, and others. Noticing your own noise is a crucial step in becoming conscious of being unconscious. This is a big deal, and it's a rich moment for you to leverage and observe both your reaction as well as your energy. Very few of us can easily move out of an emotionally charged mood while stuck in the middle of it. But now that you are becoming conscious of the thoughts, habits, and emotions anchored in your unconsciousness, the shift from being unconscious to becoming conscious happens more quickly. Here are a few actions you can take if you discover that you are indeed in the middle of an overwhelming situation, and it is running through your space:

- Disengage. Take a break, a nap, or a walk. Remove yourself physically from the situation until you regain your balance and alignment. If it is inconvenient to leave where you are, you can regain your balance by simply going to the company restroom and taking a seat there. Or push your chair away from your desk, and turn it so you create a bit of distance between you and the situation.
- Close your eyes. Check in with your Grounding Cord. Cut it off and put down a new one. Give it the command magnetically to attract to it any out-of-balance energy, or attitude that is in your experience now.

- Notice the emotions and sensations pulsing through your mind and body. With your imaginary hand, grab a bit of what is racing by and throw it down your Grounding Cord.
- Use the Rose tool for making separations from each of the others involved.
- Intentionally think about or remember something that feels better. Choose something that has absolutely nothing to do with the current predicament. When you change your thought, your mood, energy, and resulting experiences also change.
- Remind yourself that you are always okay, even if you make an 'Oops!' now and again. You are not this problem.
- Once you find your balance again, you can use the skill of discernment to identify what part of this problem you can do something about, and what is not yours to deal with.

With the tools you have been given, you have the capacity not only to rearrange your circumstances, but also to remember, empower, and align yourself. You can experience this dynamic shift that will carry you into the fifth dimensional awareness with ease and amusement.

CHAPTER TWENTY TWO

Developing Your Clairvoyance

Clairvoyance is the ability to see clearly with your inner eye. Many people regard clairvoyance with some ambivalence: either they dismiss it as a clever 'parlor trick', developed from an ability to read subtle body language and facial expressions, or they view it with a measure of awe, as some 'magical gift' that's only attainable if you happen to be the seventh son of a seventh son, for example.

The fact is we are all clairvoyant. Recognizing and developing your intuitive abilities has many practical, down-to-earth uses in one's life. In today's culture, we have access to more information than ever before. Much of it is true for someone, but it may not be accurate for you. Understanding and utilizing your intuitive abilities to discern your truth from that which is not true for you lead to a greater awareness of your own internal skills and abilities.

Employing your intuitive abilities is like having software that filters your incoming email and places those pieces you're not interested in, or don't resonate with, in the junk folder. This handy piece of software is already available to you. It came as standard equipment, bundled with your hard drive. The art is remembering it, turning that software back on, and using it.

"But wait a minute," you say. "I don't need intuition or clairvoyance. My information comes from reliable sources—magazines, the Internet, friends and family, and books. They wouldn't mislead me." Well, most likely that's correct. They may not intentionally mislead you, but their truth may not be yours. When you utilize your intuitive abilities, whether that ability is clairvoyance, telepathy or clairaudience, you will recognize whether the information given to you is aligned with your greater good long before you become entangled with it. Wouldn't your life be a whole lot easier if you had that skill? This skill already exists within you… it's just been hiding under a belief system that isn't yours! And it is not that difficult to access.

You already are intuitive

Let us give you some additional examples of how this valuable ability may benefit you:

- You will find yourself in *present time* versus in the future or past. Because you are operating in *present time* you are clearly able to see your options, as well as the appropriate response for each situation in which you find yourself.
- This clarity will increase your general awareness.
- You will begin to walk through life with Presence and Certainty. This doesn't mean in arrogance. This is a gentle, pervasive knowing that you are in management of your life.
- You will find doubt and fear begin to disappear, and your ability to take charge of your business life and personal life will increase very quickly.
- The games that you play with others, such as judgment, victim, intimidation, control, blame, competition, etc., begin to end.

- You begin to recognize and change the beliefs that you have allowed to dominate and operate in your life. Have you ever said that you sound just like your mother or father? Where do you think you learned to respond that way? *Precisely!* When you turn on your intuitive ability to see these energy patterns, they begin to change.

Intuition is as natural as breathing or eating. By making it a part of your conscious mode of operation, you will become more aligned with *who you are*. Someone once said, "Make thine eye single and you will see the light (your truth)." He was talking about clearing out all the noise that keeps you from experiencing your natural spiritual abilities, and then deliberately using them to see your own truth.

Once we have cleared out some of this noise (i.e., the untrue beliefs), we begin to see the 'light'. In other words, the light of truth (our own truth) soon becomes what we live by and what we allow to guide our decisions. The twists and turns of life become easier and less dramatic or stressful, because that inner guidance system within us is once again being utilized. It provides us with the direction to take this turn or that.

Opening to and developing your intuition and other spiritual abilities will allow you to see and experience yourself more completely. You will also discover how Capable you are.

We have put together an audio recording of an enjoyable exercise that will help you develop your clairvoyance, along with a video session from our Level 1 Program that focuses on this topic. We have also included a recording from a question and answer session that followed a recent webinar, in which one participant asked if her thoughts could have caused a plane crash.

To access these video and audio files, scan the QR code below or type the URL into your browser.

www.masteringalchemy.com/mabook-ch22-clairvoyance

CHAPTER TWENTY THREE

Relationships—
The Biggest Game on The Planet

Many of us are noticing huge changes in our relationships, and some of these changes are not at all easy to deal with. Many others are also wondering how they can best fulfill their roles as healers, teachers, and leaders, as well as what the best way might be to offer assistance to those around them. They also wonder how to consciously (and kindly) stop assisting others when those others are choosing to stay stuck and asleep.

The most fundamental changes during this Shift of Consciousness will be very personal. The primary focus is to redefine and transform how we perceive, understand, and have a relationship with every aspect of what is external to us. When we think of the word 'relationship' we think of lovers, husband and wife, child and parent. "Me in relationship to you, me in relationship to my friends, co-workers, and those I love, as well as those I dislike." There is much more to perceiving and understanding our relationship with who and what is external to us.

When the Creator said, "Go to the farthest edge of the farthest edge so that I may know myself in my fullness," you ran to the front of the line saying, "Send me!" What the Creator was actually saying was, "I wish to know myself in relationship to all that I AM." However, throughout time, as we know it, our understanding and demonstration of relationship has changed to something considerably different. We have come to know ourselves not by how we perceive *ourselves* in relationship with that which is around us, but instead, have learned to perceive our relationship to all that is around us based on what those around us *think of us*.

For example, I may not have any interest in red shirts, but all of my friends wear red shirts. Red shirts are very popular and trendy. So I give up my Seniority, and deny my own alignment with what is my truth so I may fit in. I put on a red shirt to become one with and accepted by those outside of me who are telling me what is right, and what I should and should not do. From the moment we draw our first breath to the moment we release our last, we are conditioned to define and measure ourselves by our relationship to all that is *outside* of us. We are systematically trained and conditioned by those who raise and nurture us to enter into a 'consensus reality' or 'group agreement' that many times has nothing to do with *who we are*, and everything to do with the customs and belief systems that conditioned our parents and grandparents. They were in turn influenced by the society in which they were raised, as were their parents before them.

Consensus reality is a very subtle, yet powerful influence. It structures our relationship *to* and *with* all things outside of us. More importantly, it conditions and severely limits the relationship we have with ourselves. From early childhood, we learn that what the outside world thinks of us is more important than what we each individually think of ourselves. As we grow, what we think and believe, and how we respond and behave in our third dimensional reality, is influenced and shaped by what is outside of us. Hence, almost everything about us, from our attitudes and habits, likes and dislikes, to our career choices and aspirations has its foundation in this group agreement: "Here are the rules; this is how it's done."

You are in relationship *with* everything that surrounds you. Many of us understand 'relationship' in a certain way because those outside of us have said, "This is what you should do; this is how you should move through life. This is right, that's wrong; this is truth, and this is not truth. We hang out with these people here, but we don't talk to those people over there." In other words, our *relationship to* has been conditioned from childhood. We have learned to feel the thoughts and feelings of others, and to check in with and seek approval from those around us before we act. We have learned to 'test the waters' by not fully expressing our own thoughts without first checking in to determine the acceptability of what others have to say. Notice this in your own life; it can be extremely subtle. We've learned to read other's body language to discern if it is safe to express our own desires, hopes, and dreams, before we can act on them without fear. Without realizing it, we have founded our sense of our self on the opinions and approval of others: *Am I okay? Do you approve of me? Am I acceptable in the eyes of the consensus reality?*

This too is about to change.

Contrary to everything we have been taught to believe, relationship is NOT about what other people think of you. Although this is a fundamental truth that you intellectually know, you are about to perceive this from a significantly expanded perspective. Through this understanding, you will discover that your internal relationship with yourself is the most powerful relationship you can have. From this vantage point, everything outside of you becomes a gift to relate *to* and relate *with* on your own terms. What other people think of you is none of your business.

As we have seen and read in the news, the solar flares, and coronal mass ejections (CMEs) have been bursting from the sun with rapidly increasing intensity and regularity. These are the sources of the great Waves of Light referred to throughout this book. As the Shift accelerates we are literally being showered by these Waves of Light and whether we are conscious of it or not, they are triggering enormous transformation within each of us. To reiterate, one Wave is clearing away our old memory patterns and the belief systems of the consensus reality that do not support our well-being. It is destabilizing and dissolving everything that is not aligned with our internal patterns of well-being, and our relationship to our own truths. It is therefore increasing our capacity to hold a higher Light quotient, and providing us with an opportunity to access more information, greater wisdom, and enlightenment of what we already know but have forgotten.

At the same time, another Wave is a higher dimensional vibration of Light that is providing us with the opportunity to step into Certainty, personal Power, Command, and Balance. This Wave is bringing about choices and opportunities to co-create, co-exist, and cooperate without the judgments and opinions of right/wrong, good/bad, and what you should or should not do. In the process, countless millions are experiencing significant changes in their relationships. Many are beginning to realize that they can no longer be *in relationship to* one another in the same old way. We are being given the opportunity to perceive 'relationship' through different eyes, and, in so doing, we are gaining the keys to unlock many lifetimes of conditioning that have prevented us from being able to distinguish between *who I am* and *who I am not.*

However, as this transition unfolds, many people are finding themselves in confusion. All their points of reference, all the things they were taught to trust, admire, and build their lives and beliefs upon, are destabilizing before their eyes. All our old, established third dimensional institutions are crumbling. The structures of life that feed, house and keep us safe are breaking down. Suddenly we are seeing that the very authorities that we most believed—from the healers who said, "Come to me," to the teachers who proclaimed that they have The Truth, to the leaders who said, "Trust me!" as well as all those to whom we have looked for guidance—have built their houses upon shifting sands.

As difficult as such changes may be for many, it is important to know that there IS a purpose to all that is occurring. That purpose is to shift your relationship from what is *outside* of you to an alignment with what is *inside* of you; to move from depending on the truths of others to discovering and setting your compass by your own truth. Remember, one Wave of Light is not destabilizing that which you *are*, rather, it is allowing you to clear away that which you are *not*. Your cup is emptying of all that is no longer yours. And as this occurs, the other Wave of Light is providing you with the opportunity to refill your cup. For it is with the assistance of this second Wave that the realignment of your emotional body is being altered while you sleep each night. It is through this second Wave that a more Gracious, Certain and Powerful you is being crafted. You are also beginning to remember the relationship you have with your heart and Soul. It is through this relationship that you will begin to *know yourself* and realign with who you came here to be.

Love, however, is a concept that is so vast the rational mind is not capable of perceiving its fullness. When you begin to live Love in its unique aspects of Appreciation, Gratitude, Well-being, Beauty, Kindness, Graciousness, and Certainty, these aspects literally become Living Words. And as these Living Words become internalized, a magical shift begins, initiating the activation of the living, etheric Light Body within. This is the opportunity that is unfolding right now. These are the stepping stones that will build the framework for our next level of ascension. We will discuss more about this Love in an upcoming chapter.

As the Shift continues to move us from a third dimensional consciousness to a fifth dimensional consciousness, there are a number of aspects and key concepts about relationships that we must redefine. For example, comprehending the difference between masculine and feminine energy, and understanding why becoming 'self-ish', and 'having' and 'giving' to yourself first, are some of the most important things you can do right now.

A truth about masculine and feminine energy

In the third dimension, masculine energy and feminine energy are very much out of balance. That is because most people in the third dimension do not know the rules and they don't know how to succeed at or exit the game. Knowing the rules to the games we are playing is a really big deal because relationship is the biggest game on the planet.

One of the most fundamental aspects, or rules of the relationship game is to understand masculine and feminine energy. We are not talking about male and female bodies, men and women, husband and wife, sons and daughters, or lovers. We are talking about our own internal nature and our expression of personal masculine and feminine creative energy. Regardless of our gender or sexual orientation we all have the opportunity to create by accessing the masculine and feminine energies within ourselves. However, most of us are unconscious of the great treasure we have access to, and hence do not know how to recognize and utilize these energies for our own success.

Have you ever noticed that the masculine and feminine don't quite communicate on the same wavelength? The masculine and feminine somehow seem to misconnect in this third dimensional reality. There is a very good reason for this. Let us illustrate the difference between masculine and feminine as simply as possible. We will use the concept of geometry. In a simple way, masculine energy is made up of straight lines and angles. Feminine energy is made up of curves and swirls. There are no straight lines and angles in feminine energy and there are no curves and swirls in masculine energy.

Feminine energy is very complex, energized and fast, while masculine energy is simple, uncomplicated, single-focused, and slower than feminine creative energy. By way of example, masculine energy holds about 40 points of energy and feminine energy holds about 140 points of energy. Feminine energy is very expansive, creative, and fluid. Feminine energy can do 25 things at one time while it swirls and curves. Masculine energy understands straight lines—go from point A to point B to point C and back to point A. Simple. Both types of creative energy are absolutely valuable and necessary to bring your balanced creations forth.

However, masculine energy without feminine energy is not whole; it does not feel valued; it is not nurtured or appreciated. It feels incomplete. We are not talking about men and women, and yet, yes, we are. More importantly, we are talking about your personal, internal, masculine and feminine balance. Female energy without masculine energy also is not whole. It feels unsupported; it is not focused; it is scattered, ungrounded and unstable;

it is without structure, and as a result it has no sense of direction, completion, or success.

Masculine-strong, Feminine-weak

In the third dimension, when masculine energy is out of balance it may show up in several ways. Now, make what we are about to say very personal. See if you can apply it to your own creative energy. Please hear the words and also read between the lines. When the masculine energy feels as if it is not good enough, when it is in fear, when it has been told it will never succeed, it is not worth anything, and it has no value, it is off balance. To compensate, the masculine energy may demonstrate a false strength. It may puff itself up and say, "I have these great ideas and these big dreams; I want to lead and create. I know what I'm doing. Follow me." When a female who also is in fear and is weak, timid or withdrawn finds this puffed up male, it is a perfect match. She can remain in her false weakness and neediness, and he can remain in his false strength. Neither is challenged to change. Remember, the Law of Attraction gives each of them exactly what they are asking for. As it plays out, however, it will look something like this.

In your mind draw a straight line and then make an angled line moving off of that first line. (See the diagram.) The masculine energy leads: "Come with me. I know what I am doing. I have this great dream. I am going to build this wonderful house for you in Toronto, Canada." And the feminine energy says, "Oh, this is so wonderful. I also want a big house in Toronto." The masculine and feminine start out together at the first point of the line, and the masculine goes forth to construct the house and the feminine, because feminine has curves and swirls, begins to create. She selects new paint, new drapes, and designs the landscaping. She is thrilled and satisfied that she will get to create her nest.

The masculine continues forward and then his habits of fear and self-doubt pop up. The masculine hesitates and becomes afraid of failing: *I don't know what to do because I am told that I am hopeless. I am not going to succeed. I am not worth anything,* and the masculine doubts his ability and stops moving forward on building in Toronto. The masculine has built 80% of the new home. He has traveled 80% down that line and then he says, "No I think we should move to a tropical climate. It will be much nicer, and we can have a house on the beach in Hawaii. I know what is best. Follow me to Hawaii."

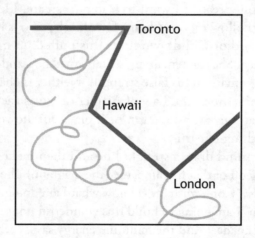

The feminine energy is out there swirling around in Toronto and must now stop creating. She is now incomplete. She isn't able to complete her plans. The feminine energy says, "Oh. Well, okay.

A tropical beach would be nice. I would love a beach house in Hawaii. I love you and trust you." And they move, but she is incomplete. He is also incomplete, but he begins to build the house in Hawaii. Again the feminine swirls and it curves and begins to have fun creating in Hawaii. She buys the bamboo flooring and plants the hibiscus flowers.

Then once again, when he gets deeply into the process, the off-balance masculine says: "Well, I think I need to change my job, which means we have to move to London. Come with me to London and we can have the beach house some other day." Once again the female energy is incomplete and unsatisfied. The masculine energy drives the game and the feminine energy continues to give up her power. If the feminine has even just a small portion of her truth still available, she will begin to get frustrated, angry, and maybe resentful. The feminine creativity is being dampened because she was very excited about the big house in Toronto and then the beach house. She was getting very creative because that is what feminine energy does. The masculine energy is also incomplete in this example, and must find his inner truth to make any change.

Does this dynamic remind you of anyone? Notice it within yourself or within someone you know. This person would have great dreams and plans and have an attitude of bravado. They would enjoy, for a short time, both the masculine and feminine creative energies as they build the house and design the landscape successfully together. At some point, their fears and weakness would arise to sabotage their path and soon excuses and 'better ideas' would be followed instead.

Now let's take a look at some of the other permutations.

Feminine-Strong, Masculine-Weak

If you reverse the roles discussed above, and have a relationship in which the feminine energy is very strong, and the masculine energy is weaker, it is as if the feminine energy says: "I have these grand dreams and desires. I wish to have this… I want that… I would like to have these other things over here." But sometimes beneath this apparent strength and determination, there also is *I cannot have*, *I don't deserve nice things*, or *I can't receive*. Feminine creative energy without the balance and structure of masculine energy is very scattered and undependable. It is as if you pour water onto the surface of the table, and it simply spreads everywhere; it is not contained, focused or directed. There is no structure (cup) in place to hold the feminine creative power.

When this off-balance feminine asks of the masculine, "Oh, I want you to build me a house," the masculine says, "I'd love to build you a house. I am a carpenter. I can do this for you." And he goes off in his excitement and gets the wood, stone and electrical wiring and begins to build a beautiful house. This is the creativity of straight lines and angles discussed earlier.

In the meantime, the feminine energy has continued creating. After asking for a house, she went off to yoga class, tea with friends, shopping at the mall. She bought the ingredients for a gourmet dinner (notice the curves and swirls of creativity), went to a math lecture and tried on new running shoes. When she finally brings her attention back home, she greets the masculine, and she asks, "What are you doing?"

"Well, dear," says the confused masculine energy, "I am building the house you said you wanted."

And the feminine energy either responds with, "I did? When did I say that?" Or "Oh, I know, but I've changed my mind. What

I really want is to move to Hawaii and have a beach house there."

"Oh. Okay, then. I can build you a house at the beach." He says.

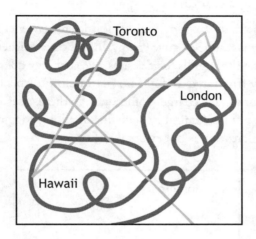

"That would be so wonderful," the feminine energy replies. Off they go, and the story repeats itself. With this ungrounded, scattered pattern, the masculine energy feels invalidated, unappreciated, and unheard. This scattered feminine energy is swirling all around in an unmanaged manner, and the masculine energy follows her, or tries to, never coming to completion. When she changes her mind again and again, the masculine also changes his direction for her, trying to build a house, a structure within which she can be happy and create. However, with this pattern, both the feminine and masculine creative energies are incomplete, and over time, frustration sets in. Do you know someone like this? This person is ungrounded and does not complete the many projects they have begun, because they are busily dreaming up even more ideas. They may also have saved all the materials and supplies they collected for each of these projects... for years, promising to get to them someday.

Feminine-Weak, Masculine-Weak

There is also the pattern of weak feminine creative energy, together with weak masculine creative energy. In this case, neither is creating easily and neither fulfills their desires. Weak energy does not create. It gets very frustrated and has no permission to speak up, to set direction, or to take charge. Sometimes, in these cases, neither the masculine, nor the feminine can define or ask for their desires. The first step of creation is not even taken.

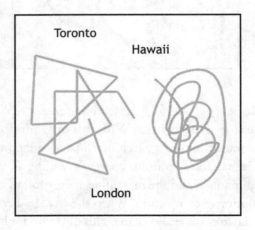

The masculine energy doesn't build the structure for the feminine to create within, and the feminine doesn't define what she wants him to build. You may recognize this creation pattern in those around you. Decisions never seem to get made and they change their minds frequently. There is no forward movement. Inertia can occur. Both want the other to make the decision of what movie to go to, and soon it is too late; all the good movies have already come and gone. As a personal exploration, you might become aware of this dynamic demonstrated in the lives of those around you and, ultimately, in your own creative process. Do you know someone who exhibits inertia and is not creating fully in a way that you know they have the potential to create? Perhaps they don't take risks and use vocabulary that is self-defeating?

Feminine-Strong, Masculine-Strong

The flip side of this is a creation pattern of strong, feminine energy and strong, masculine energy. Again, both are in fear and, internally, both feel a great deal of confusion, pressure to perform, and insecurity. There will be a great deal of competition, pushing and shoving, incompletion and turmoil.

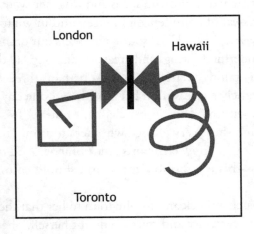

Both creative powers here can be uncompromising and stubborn. Consequently, both dig in their heels and nothing gets created. You may know people who do this in their creative space. They may boast and brag and present themselves as confident and accomplished, but in actuality, have achieved remarkably little in their lives. This person may 'know it all' and argue with every suggestion others make. They often blame and demonstrate anger at others. It is the fault of "others" that they don't succeed.

How did we get so out of whack?

When your masculine creative energy is too weak or too strong, and/or your feminine creative energy is too weak or too strong, we call this the third dimensional relationship game. This is where most of us have learned to be and to live our lives. How did we get here, in this off balance state? Here is an example: There is a little girl (or little boy) who is very talented, skilled, and knowledgeable. She is very excited about who she is and what she wants to do. She has a great deal of confidence in herself and in what is possible. She simply says, "I can!" This little child sets out on her path and creates wonderful drawings and great art. She sings all the time and passionately builds amazing things. At perhaps three years of age, she is extremely successful in her world, and one day says to her favorite grown-up, "Look at my elephant I drew." It is a beautiful elephant, and she is very pleased with her creation. The grown-up says, "Don't you know elephants aren't orange? And besides, this isn't right—this is a scribbly mess. You should color inside the lines."

This is such a shock and invalidation to her that the little child drops out of certainty and starts to doubt herself. She steps away from her power. The *you're not okay* belief slides right into that little slot where *I'm great and successful* used to be just a moment ago. At first, the little child is confused, and then she does one of two things. She may say, "Well, I'll show you," and goes through the rest of her life working to prove that she is good. She may become a Type A personality, and an over-achiever in order to show that long-ago grown-up that she really is of value. However, there is still a little doubt. There is an *Am I really okay?* that sits in her space and among her beliefs about herself. She has private thoughts like *I am not sure whether this painting I just did is actually worth ten thousand dollars,* even though on the outside she presents herself as absolutely confident, determined, and strong. She is paid her ten thousand dollars over and over again, yet she still doubts her ability and worth.

The other possible reaction this little child may have is: *Well, maybe that grown-up was right. Maybe I'm not that good after all.* She never returns to that powerful, talented expression she once had. This passionate child grows up to doubt her every decision. She hides, worries, and does not take risks. She never draws (or sings or dances or creates) again.

Every one of us has experienced the result of this distorted feminine-masculine creative energy. Once you understand the distinctions, and the power of these creative energies, you will be better able to balance them and, therefore, create more powerfully from that fullness. Then, when you step into a relationship, you will continue to hold the belief that you count, you can make a difference, and you have value. There will be no push or shove, no competition or invalidation, and no better or worse. There is a balance between and within your masculine and feminine ways of creating. Once balanced, you will recognize yourself and move forward into joyfully painting those elephants any color you choose with playmates that celebrate with you. We, and the world of art, are very happy that Picasso never believed his critical relatives.

We have now defined masculine creative energy (straight lines and angles) and feminine creative energy (swirls and curves), and we now know what happens when those creative energies are out of balance with each other; when one is dominant and one is weak. (Please remember, we are talking about your personal creative energy here, not bodies and genders.) We have also discovered how each of us gets into this place of misalignment. As we continue to move through this Shift and transition, it is absolutely essential that the masculine nature and the feminine nature in each of us be brought into balance. This rebalancing is very possible. As we choose to step up into these higher aspects of consciousness we naturally include and anchor greater levels of personal power and alignment with All That Is.

When your masculine and feminine creative energies are aligned, balanced, and playing well together, you are, by default, in higher fourth and fifth dimensional states of being. So, to briefly review: higher vibrational words such as Ease, Laughter, Community, Co-creation, Respect, Admiration, Appreciation, and Balance are only experienced when we are in the higher fourth dimension. Whereas denser, slower words like competition, depression, guilt, blame, and victim, are only experienced when we are in the third and lower fourth dimensions. In the higher fourth and fifth dimensions, there is no lack. There are no limitations. There are no 'shoulds' or 'should nots', and you cannot do anything 'wrong' there. Elephants can indeed be orange.

When healthy masculine energy is in relationship with healthy feminine energy, masculine creativity has the room and the opportunity to come up with new ideas and build new structures.

He now has the motivation and the impetus to learn, grow, and expand into new realms of possibility. He feels validated, and has the support to explore new houses that he can build in which the feminine can create. And because healthy masculine energy also loves balanced female energy, he then says, "How can I uplift, nurture, and provide for this feminine creativity? How can I assist her in creating her dreams? Together we can create new worlds." This co-creating occurs within each of us, in our individual expressions as well as our external relationships. The man builds the raised garden beds and the woman plants and tends the vegetables and herbs. We're sure you've seen two (or more) people come together and do some wonderful things as a team.

When healthy feminine creative energy is balanced and in alignment with the healthy masculine, she has the structure and scaffolding necessary for creativity. She can easily and passionately design, plan, execute, and bring to fruition her dreams. She can fully focus on her studies and research; her writing and craft; the music and math that she loves so well. Balanced masculine energy provides the necessary structure, dependability, and stability. It is reliable. There is a focus, strength, and a sense of stability for the feminine energy to experience itself safely and with permission. When feminine energy is safe and has permission, it is expansive and creative. The masculine creates a container or field that offers the feminine a dependable space in which to create and be happy. It is from this balance that a flow unfolds. It is then that the feminine can say, "I would like a house."

And the masculine energy smiles and says: "I can happily build this for you. How big and what color?"

There is then a give and take, a cooperation and co-creation. The feminine says, "What you have built is wonderful. Can we build a garden also? Is it possible to add a couple of birdhouses too? And what about…?"

As the feminine creates more widely, the masculine expands the structure to make plenty of room for her swirls and curves. There is balance. There is the shared thrill of creating in passion together. As an example in our life together, Jim happily built a trellis for Roxane, and she is happily planting the tomatoes.

In this higher fourth dimensional balance, this combined creative energy becomes very powerful and has the capacity simply to look at the third dimensional world and say, "I hear your opinion of me not being worthy. Thank you very much. AND that is not where I choose to go." There is no discussion or negotiation. No energy is thrown, and no one is invalidated. You make your choice, then dust off your sandals and set about your business, allowing that other person the room to go about theirs.

Bringing your masculine and feminine energy into alignment

It is of utmost importance during this time of Shift to identify, experience, and begin to anchor healthy masculine and feminine energy into your creative process. Words are an easy place to begin to rewire your masculine and feminine creative energy into balance.

Let us give you an example of the shift in alignment these masculine and feminine words bring forth within you. Be playful with this. As with everything we offer, there is no right or wrong way of having this experience.

As mentioned earlier, masculine words have straight lines and angles. When you become or wear a masculine word as a coat, or as an energy in your space, you will have a feeling or sense of the straight lines and angles. Feminine words will give you a sense of curves and swirls. A word that has a masculine nature to it would be, for example, the word, Capable. This doesn't mean there isn't a feminine version of the word Capable. We will talk more about this later.

- Take a breath and feel the feeling of being Capable. No one's opinion counts here but yours.
- Take another breath and feel within your body the *strength* and alignment of being Capable. Capable is the structure and scaffolding upon which much more can be built. You may notice that your body might want to sit up straight; your head may want to go back. Your shoulders may want to move back. It is a sense of *Yes, I am Capable.*
- Allow yourself simply to feel and explore this. Make it up at first if you have to. Capable, in this case, has a structure to it. It can be felt as a masculine word. Feel its stability.
- Now add to Capable the vibration and feeling of being Certain about yourself. Is there anything that you do well? Can you brush your teeth? Are you Certain? Can you do it every time? *Yes, absolutely! I am Capable and Certain.*
- Let your body *be* and *feel* these two words. Let them create the structure or container (masculine) within which feminine creativity can experience itself. Without the structure and container, feminine words and creative energy flow out in a scattered way, with no direction, like water poured upon the table.

- Now find the feeling of Ease. Ease is like an exhale. This word has a more feminine energy in it. Notice that Ease has no structure to it. Would you let your attention Focus (masculine) on Ease while you are being Certain and Capable. All of us have masculine and feminine creativity within us.
- Certain, Capable, Ease. Let yourself experience the feminine flow, and would you not only feel Ease but would you also like yourself. *I like me* has no boundaries, no edges, no lines and no angles. *I like me!*
- Now give yourself Permission. Permission has no lines either. It is *Wow! I can do this.* You are building a (masculine) container of Certain, Focus, and Capable to allow (feminine) Ease and Permission to express themselves.
- Find the vibration of Kindness, which is another very powerful and very feminine word.
- One last word: Allow Appreciation to begin to flow within your space. Allow yourself to Appreciate the Capability and Certainty that you now have Permission to experience. Allow it to be very Focused.

Here are some other suggestions

Create lists of masculine and feminine words

Create separate lists of masculine and feminine words and wear one of each every day. Experiment.

Also, begin to play by choosing a masculine word and finding the feminine aspect of it. You might quickly recognize the straight lines and angles of Certainty, but see if you can recognize the feminine aspect of that word too. The feminine might demonstrate Certainty when the row of lettuce she just planted is sure to germinate. The feminine word, Gentle, also has a masculine aspect. A Gentle masculine energy may be like a grandfather, holding the infant. Get the picture?

As you progress through this work, you will begin to discern both masculine and feminine energies in words and bring them into your awareness as aspects of the totality of *who you are*. Working with the words and balancing your masculine and feminine energies are enjoyable and expedient ways to accomplish the rewiring and the remembering of *who you really are*. They are also foundational pieces for the entire online program we teach, which you have partial access to throughout this book.

Becoming aware in your daily life of how you create

Begin to consciously and intentionally incorporate both feminine and masculine creativity. For example, if you have an important project at work—designing a new marketing campaign, for instance—it is essential (using your masculine creative energy) to analyze and understand the budget you have to work within and the costs of print and online advertising. It is also crucial to understand the size and resolution specifications required for each of these types of advertising. If you simply rushed into creatively designing ads (feminine), without the understanding and structure (masculine) of the system, you might have a beautiful but useless piece of advertising art. Create the structure or foundation first, then you can happily, successfully create within it.

Cycles of feminine and masculine

There are cycles upon cycles within this evolution of humanity. We have a cycle called day and night, which is created by the Moon orbiting the Earth. We have a cycle called seasons, and another called a year; the time it takes the Earth to go around the sun. There's also a bigger cycle that occurs as a result of the precession of the equinoxes, when the Sun's position at the vernal equinox shifts backwards through the centuries. It completes a full circle in 26,000+ years.

In the precession of the equinoxes, there are two very specific cycles, or phases. The first approximately 13,000+ years is considered to be a predominantly masculine energy cycle, and the second 13,000+ years is a predominantly feminine energy cycle. Many things happen during that first 13,000-year cycle. During that part of the cycle, the feminine energy goes into a resting phase, and the masculine energy takes over. This masculine cycle creates structure, safety, and permission in many ways. Then it rests, and the feminine creative aspect moves to the forefront and more creation occurs, until it's time to rest again and allow the masculine energy to bring the creations of the feminine into effect. This continues throughout each phase and cycle through the ages. This is not something we typically pay attention to because it is bigger than a day, a week and a year.

With the Shift that is occurring, we have now reached a point where the present, masculine, phase is about to end, and instead of continuing as we have in the third dimension with alternating masculine and feminine cycles, we are moving into a new cycle of consciousness. This is one in which masculine and feminine become one balanced, unified field of consciousness. In order to enter and hold yourself in the vibrations of a fifth dimensional reality and bring the unified field into wholeness, the masculine and the feminine within you must be in balance. When this is accomplished, the structure of the masculine creative energy begins to be the container in which the feminine creative energy can grow and expand. The feminine energy can then direct the masculine energy into expanded structure, which in turn allows the feminine to create within that new space. It's an ongoing ebbing and flowing of masculine and feminine that allows for amazing opportunities and a joyful creative process. This new level of balanced masculine and feminine creative energies is where we are headed.

You are big. You have never been small, and you have always been the little child who was Capable and talented with Certainty and Ease. You just simply let a grown-up talk you out of it for a moment. Now that moment is over. Right now you are Certain, Capable and Focused. You are in Appreciation with Permission and Ease again. And orange elephants are coming back into style.

I like me—just like you did as that little child.

As you balance this masculine and feminine creative energy and begin to choose which to use in each situation, the world around you will change significantly. It is all about you. You are the center of your universe, and when you begin to choose consciously how you wish to create, you will find that the Light that you hold becomes so magnetic that your service to others will be effortless. Your personal growth will be boundless.

On the following page you'll find a QR Code and the URL to a page with two audio recordings. The first features questions and answers on various aspects of relationships and love, including love of family and friends, and love as expressed in a traditional marriage. The second recording is designed to help you bring your masculine and feminine energies into alignment.

WHAT DO YOU MEAN THE THIRD DIMENSION IS GOING AWAY?

www.masteringalchemy.com/mabook-ch23-relationships

CHAPTER TWENTY FOUR

How to Create a Hot, Healthy, Higher Relationship

Have you ever fallen in love? Falling in love is a third dimensional phenomenon and is one of the many ways we forget *who we are*. When we are 'in love', many of us lose our focus, we lose our purpose, we lose sight of our goals, and we lose our passion. We begin to blend with that other person and we lose our identity. Then one day we wake up and realize with a jolt, *Wait a minute, I've lost me! I've given up all my favorite activities, my hobbies, my friends, because I was so consumed in my relationship that I forgot about these things, or pushed them aside. I gave up me for we.* It's similar to when you see couples who wear the same shirts, walk the same dogs, or have exactly the same likes, dislikes and opinions—they have become so much like one another, their identities have blurred, leaving them with very little individual identity of their own. When we are in a vibrational resonance, or matching energy with someone, we often get into what's called 'sympathetic resonance'. It is similar to when you tap a tuning fork and another one on the other side of the room starts vibrating in harmonic resonance with the first one.

What often happens is that when people fall in love, they fall into a third dimensional group agreement that says, "I like you, because you're like me. We have commonality; we have mutual purpose, we have all these same vibrations in our fields." Your personality and your vibrational truths line up with their vibrational truths—sympathetic resonance. Over time, however, many of us find that the things that really interested us about that person begin to lose their significance. Now we have the things we wanted in a partner on a daily basis, we begin to take our attention off them and stop appreciating them. What was exciting and interesting about our partner has perhaps become a habit or commonplace and just part of the furniture. *Life* has happened around you, and a degree of mediocrity crept in between you.

For example, let's say you really want a spouse that helps out around the house, one that never forgets to take the garbage out. Taking the garbage out, in your perception, is a sign that your spouse really loves and cares for you. You also want him/her to play tennis and golf with you. You believe that sharing activities, and likes and dislikes means the two of you get on well, are a good match and enjoy being together. So that's the kind of partner you marry. He/she takes the garbage out every day, and is happy to play tennis and golf with you whenever you want. Time passes; taking the garbage out becomes a habit, and pretty soon you've taken your attention off it. You start to forget that taking the garbage out was proof of your partner's love for you; you don't value it any more. More time passes and you don't play tennis and golf together very often, and then not at all. You both start doing other things, and all of a sudden one or both of you realize, *I'm not like you any more, but I made this commitment that was forever and ever, and I can't bring myself to break that.*

How many times have you met couples that absolutely should no longer be in relationship? They had a moment—regardless of what length of time the moment was—and it served them both very well. But they were so locked into the original, cultural agreement of 'falling in love and getting married', that when it was no longer serving either of them, they agreed to give up and stay stuck in mediocrity, or move on and continue the 'falling in love' pattern with someone else with identical results.

Here's another example of a lower dimensional relationship phenomenon. Have you ever had one of those 'eyes across a crowded room' moments? You looked at someone and immediately thought: *That's the one! I've got to have that one right now!* And he/she looked back at you with the same intensity in their eyes. Suddenly there was an undeniable level of passion (sexual energy) running through and between your body and theirs. Nothing and no one else existed in the room. All logic, wisdom and ideals—everything—was overrun by that intense, magnetic vibration. This is called 'falling in lust'. Consumed with the thought of having each other, you both escape into the nearest empty room. You then spend several days rolling around with entangled arms, legs and body parts. You have a peak sexual adventure. Waking up the next morning/afternoon/week, after your twentieth massive orgasm, you roll over and look at that other person and think…

What the heck was I thinking?

Both of these are examples of how we can become so engaged with how the external makes us feel inside that we attribute those good feelings as *coming from* or being *attached to* that other person. We believe that person is the cause of those grand feelings inside us. Nothing could be further from the truth; however, the cultural, group-agreement has convinced us otherwise. We tend to lose our own focus and our relationship to the energy that is our own personal, internal alignment. We begin to believe we must either fall in love or in lust to feel those feelings and that energy of connection.

Being self-ish

Higher dimensional relationships are quite different from what most of us typically experience in the third dimension. The tacit agreements and structures that were the foundation of many relationships in the past are no longer relevant when one lives on the platforms of higher awareness. The rigid structures of the third dimension serve us very well until we choose to step outside that box. As the Shift continues to unfold, more of us are asking big questions and choosing to be 'picky', to not 'settle for', and to surround ourselves only with the people and situations that vibrate where we are and where we know we want to be.

The concept of 'selfish' in the third dimension can mean greed, conceit, competition, worry and separation from others. Many times it includes emotions such as jealousy, competition, resentment and fear. Selfish people cannot have intimate, long-term relationships, and are generally unhealthy and unhappy. They are continually looking over their shoulder for ways to cheat others and get more for themselves. Not a fun way to live. Selfish in the higher dimensions, however, is an important requirement for healthy, mutually supportive relationships. So let us reframe the term.

Self-ish means being all about yourself—you are the center of the universe. When self-ish, you are continually focused upon what works for you, what is aligned with your inner guidance and what is the most integrity-filled thing you can do in any situation. A self-ish person only does what feels good inside. Their well-being is of top priority. Competition, and worrying about who and what others are, compared to you, simply doesn't feel aligned. When a person is standing on the platform of higher consciousness, greed and separation is not even an option. Their focus is on themselves. *How do I make myself a better person? Would I feel good inside if I said that thing to her? How can I help that man, without giving my seniority away? What do I need to do and change to make myself more connected with Source and humanity?* When someone is self-ish and is taking care of their needs and goals first, their cup is abundantly full; hence they have much, much more to share with others. 1+1=3 can only occur between healthy, self-ish, self-aware individuals who are aligned with their internal guidance system. Selfish in the third dimension, however, is surrounded by lack, doubt and fear.

In a healthy relationship, each person must be very aware of their internal guidance system and have the ability to discern their truth from the truths of others. They must also know their boundaries and how to say "No thank you," gracefully. Being able to do this for yourself first enables you naturally and effortlessly to allow others the same freedom. When you know what pleases you, and you can hold your space, you have more ability to allow others simply to be who, and where, they are on their path. No competition. When you are not self-ish in this higher way, you have the tendency to step outside of what you know is in alignment, do what you don't want to do, and become a resentful victim. Can you identify someone like this in your life? Holding this energy long enough will affect their well-being and cause illness and disease. No one wants a partner, spouse or friend like this.

Look at it this way: Imagine you are in the scorching hot desert with a group of nine others whom you may or may not know, and you are the only one with a canteen of water. How would you feel if you passed your canteen around to them before drinking from it first? Most of us would be worried and concerned that they would drink all the water before the canteen made its way back to us, and we would be left thirsting. Now imagine how you would feel if you drank from it first, then shared it with them.

The flight attendant says, "Put the oxygen mask on yourself first, then assist the person beside you." If you don't, you may suffocate while trying to help them. Take care of yourself first and you will have the life and breath to assist others.

Me Bubbles and We Bubbles

When two self-ish, whole individuals meet to play, they bring with them all the richness of *who they fully are*. They have and continue to work on releasing their own 'stuff' and, therefore, there is less baggage, positioning and game playing. They both have learned to be honest with themselves and, therefore, can be honest with each other. Each of them likes, appreciates and even loves themselves first, and can now do likewise with others. In other words, they each have a strong, complete Me Bubble that is filled with all the wonderful aspects of *who they are* and what they enjoy, so when they join neither loses any aspects of their bubble, nor takes from the other.

When two whole Me Bubbles meet, a third Bubble is created where they share their commonalities without giving up or losing *who they are*. This new Bubble (see illustration) is the new world they have the potential of creating together. This is where they bring their great gifts and skills together to co-create. Each individual contributes to and receives from their We Bubble as they desire. What they create together, whether it's a garden, a business or a baby, is wildly successful and fun. Their We Bubble can be of any size, and the size fluctuates as the relationship develops, grows and changes. This is the place where they can freely play together. This is where the dynamic of 1+1=3 is best demonstrated. They can create more together than they can separately. Within your We Bubble you can have many other Bubbles. For instance, within our We Bubble, we have a Business Bubble, a Garden Bubble and a Snowshoeing Bubble, among other adventures.

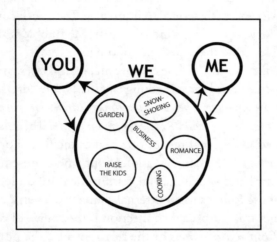

As you live more fully in the higher dimensions, as you are selfish and develop your Me Bubble, more of your relationships will be with individuals who also understand relationship from this Bubble concept. Those relationships that are not a match to you will simply fade away. As you walk your path, many old friends and family will disappear from your life. You have a choice to see this as a sad moment, or as validation that the personal work you've been doing is working. Your Me Bubble is stronger and more whole. Those you attract now will be playmates of a new, higher dimensional caliber.

I love me when I'm with you

When the two individuals above enter into an intimate relationship, much about it is different from relationships experienced in the dense, rigid third dimension. They enter it with well-practiced energy tools, plus a more balanced, personal commitment to their own growth and their service to humanity. They both continue to grow and develop a whole and successful Me Bubble while allowing and respecting the experience of others.

Third dimensional feelings of love are, many times, attached to the individual's need for something external. *I love him because he takes out the garbage. She cares for the children. He makes money for us to live. She is smart. He says he loves me.* The relationship is described in external terms. She makes me feel happy. She is my 'better half'. There is confusion about where those feelings of love originate and where they are felt. In the third dimension, we connect those feelings to an external source—a lover, a child, etc. Many times this misplaced connection is the source of confusion and the *I am not okayness* of the relationship. The potential of Love, however, is much greater, and once we understand this, a very different experience becomes available.

Love, as a feeling, is experienced within you. It is not a need to be satisfied. It is not because he takes out the garbage, or she earns the income. Love is a personal, internal feeling that is experienced within you. It is not something that you can give to or receive from another. It isn't possible to *give* Love. Relationship is the most challenging game there is. *I love you* has many culturally programed aspects, most of which lead to confusion, discomfort and misunderstanding.

What if we recognize that *I love you* from the external expression is more accurately: *I love me when I am with you?* How would our relationships be different? *I am enjoying myself in your presence, or when I think of you.* Love, as a feeling, is an internal affair. This changes the focus entirely. This new perspective allows Love to be experienced in many expanded, personal ways.

When your partner smiles and you say, "I love you," you are not expressing what is occurring outside of you. You are, instead, expressing the aspect of Love called Appreciation, and it is within you. *I feel good inside (I love me) when you smile. Because it feels so good inside, I want to do everything I can to make you smile more often.* The feeling of love and all its permutations is about you. It's an internal, personal experience within you. When this is understood and chosen as a way of life by both parties, life together takes on very different dimensions.

During their summer vacation in New York, the woman says, "That necklace is so beautiful." He smiles and returns to the store to buy it for her December holiday present. He then gets to experience the pleasure and excitement inside himself about his surprise for the next six months!

"I would really like to ski in Aspen someday," the man says, flipping through a magazine. She secretly arranges a week's skiing trip for him and his best friend for the following winter. She is pleased and in love with herself as her surprise continues to grow and unfold over many months. *I love me when I am with you.*

From this platform, a new and expanded awareness begins. Because love is an internal, personal feeling, *I love me when I walk in the woods. I love me when I watch the sunset. I love me when I hear others laugh. I love me when the cat on my lap is purring. I love me when I see the tomatoes sprouting in my garden.* You begin to become more conscious that you are in relationship WITH all things around you—the cat, tomatoes, sunset and trees. This opens a new awareness that Love, as your own internal experience, allows other feelings such as Appreciation, Gratitude, Respect, Ease, and Presence to be experienced as Love also. *I love me* opens unlimited possibilities in the most wonderful and unexpected ways.

This higher dimensional Love is the natural result of creating and living your life wearing the seven Living Words. When you feel Certain, Happy and Gracious, for example, you also have an *inner smile*, and you like yourself regardless of what the world around you is experiencing. You are pleased with yourself and can allow others to be in their chosen state of well-being (or non-well-being) and not judge them or want to meddle in their experience. You are, however, very available to them if they ask.

As you are able to more continuously remain in the energy of self-appreciation, you automatically attract others of the same vibration. When your new friend smiles and demonstrates their enthusiasm, you also smile and feel the love in your life. When you are enjoying your partner's laughter, there is nothing you would do to interfere with their happiness and fun. Their joy allows you to love yourself that much more. In fact, you enjoy discovering new ways to please them because when they are happy, you are happy, and because *I love me when I'm with you.*

On the following page you will find a QR Code and URL that will take you to an audio recording featuring questions and answers on the subject of higher dimensional relationships to enhance your understanding of what we covered in this chapter.

HOW TO CREATE A HOT, HEALTHY, HIGHER RELATIONSHIP

www.masteringalchemy.com/mabook-ch24-higher-relationships

CHAPTER TWENTY FIVE

Sympathy, Empathy and Compassion

The third dimensional chakras operate as barometers of balance or imbalance. If you know what they do, you will have an opportunity to refocus your attention and begin to realign yourself. All seven major chakras support us, but for most of us, the lower three chakras guide the life we experience.

- **FIRST CHAKRA:** Survival—The first chakra's job is to keep you safe so that you may fulfill your purpose in this lifetime. If you are threatened and it's not the exit point of your life, the first chakra overrides everything to keep you safe. It will activate the flight or fight mechanism and cause you to jump back onto the curb before the bus hits you. The first chakra is located at the lowest tip of your spine.

- **SECOND CHAKRA:** Emotions—The second chakra deals with the lower emotions (neediness, jealousy, resentment, addictions, and grief) plus sexuality and sensuality. This chakra is located two finger's width below your navel and back toward the spine.

- **THIRD CHAKRA:** Power—Solar Plexus. The third chakra deals with power, control, judgment, and resistance. If you find your solar plexus region in pain, it may not be acid indigestion. This chakra is telling you that you are out of balance, in a push-and-shove (power and control) situation. If you are resisting or judging something at a high enough degree, the third chakra area will be blocked and/or in pain.

Together, the lower three chakras support sympathy and empathy. These two third dimensional reactions are based on past experiences. They tell you where you are in relation to your safety and to fitting in emotionally, as well as in relation to your well-being, and to how you are accepted by others. This is the job of empathy and sympathy.

Empathy

Empathy is the ability to feel the emotional and physical pain others are experiencing. Many new age lightworkers take great pride in and are glamorized by their ability to feel others' pain physically. They see it as a useful way to read the energy of others and to heal them. Eventually, by continuing to choose to bring pain into your body, you will damage your health and well-being. Carrying pain will increase your aging process and wear you down.

Empathy is also a second chakra, third dimensional means of determining if the person who stands before you is safe for you to interact with. The second chakra reads the energy of the other person to determine their mood, attitude, emotional/mental stability, and to determine whether being near them is safe. It is the job of your first chakra, not your second, to keep you and your body safe. Using your second chakra for this job (empathy) becomes a burden and interferes with your well-being and balance.

Sympathy

Sympathy is the internal, third dimensional, emotional reaction to observing another's pain. You feel sorry, concerned, sad, worried and troubled by what they are going through. Sympathy is not feeling their pain in your body; it is a lower second chakra reaction to it, felt within your emotional body. The habit of sympathy will destroy your emotional balance and eventually your physical well-being also.

Neither sympathy, nor empathy will benefit your friend in pain. The pain on their path exists for them to leverage for their greater personal mastery. Nothing you can worry about, feel or take on for them will positively affect their journey.

Compassion

Compassion, on the other hand, is an upper fourth dimensional expression. It operates in the *present time* moment and allows you to neutrally, objectively observe the situation that is before you. It is nonjudgmental. It is allowing and accepting of things exactly as they are. The act of being in your Higher Mind and within your Octahedron offers you the ability to be compassionate. Facing your friend who is in pain while you are in this compassionate space, gives you the room to see and offer the wise, helpful information they can benefit from if they choose to.

Conversely, when you are in the third dimensional reactions of sympathy and empathy it is impossible for you to guide and mentor your friend. Compassion allows you to observe without becoming entangled in the drama, emotional reactions, and physical pain of others. This place of power then enables you to be of greater service. You can assist others to release their unbeneficial patterns, beliefs and habits in greater ways—if they wish to do so.

Reaction versus response

For many, the coming months and years of the Shift will be very confusing and emotional. Those who rely on reactionary patterns of sympathy and empathy to understand or help others will experience a charged, emotional and physical, electromagnetic pull into those people's feelings, thoughts, and pain. Let us say that again: As the momentum of the Shift continues to increase, if you choose to rely on empathy and sympathy you will find these charged electromagnetic patterns pulling you into the erratic, unfocused, painful feelings, thoughts and drama of those standing before you.

Most of us can clearly remember where we were and what we were doing when we heard about the events of 9/11. As the event unfolded, two ripples of energy moved around the world:

- A third dimensional reaction steeped in fear
- A fourth dimensional response that stepped up and asked, "What can I do? How can I help?"

The people in the New York area first experienced the third dimensional reaction of fear, followed by the second response, which moved many into a fourth dimensional vibration of compassion, which involved no thinking and no conditions. Some friends of ours hung their landline phone out the window so others might call home and offered their bathroom to the fire fighters. All that mattered was that well-being be brought back into balance. Communities joined together to serve and assist. Others around the world were also affected by these events. Many who were not even directly involved felt empathy and sympathy and chose to feel physical and emotional discomfort, which also included fear, tears and worry. Many others chose compassion, and in their own way stepped up to help. How did you respond at the time?

Both reacting and responding are very available choices during this time of Shift. You have this choice every moment. Remembering and using your tools to stay focused, observant, clear and purposeful will allow you to hold a vibrational tone that keeps you well above the reactions of the lower three chakras and out of the third dimensional fear.

CHAPTER TWENTY SIX

More on The Power of Words to Rewire

The Living Words are a tool we covered in the previous section, yet there is a great deal more to them than what has been presented. Words are very important components of the flow of creation. Certain words amplify, others shift, and some halt the flow of creation. Adjectives and adverbs increase or shape it. As you become conscious of being conscious, you begin to recognize that before the word was spoken there was the thought. There were also feelings, and there were vibrations and frequencies—all of which are energy.

The fifth dimension is structured in frequencies that promote and hold tremendous alignment and well-being. When you are aligned with this flow, your access to All That Is becomes unlimited. The more harmonic resonance and alignment there is, the simpler it is to create. From a third dimensional perspective, the simplest way to align with these fifth dimensional frequencies is by becoming and demonstrating the vibration, or feeling, of selected words while maintaining your point of observation. This will allow you to shift your relationship to the world around you from one of reaction to one that allows you to choose how you wish to create and manage your experience.

The words you hold, consciously or unconsciously, collectively create a vibrational tone that is unique to you. You become known by your tone. *She is sad and unpleasant to be around; he is always angry and upset.* As you become aligned with the higher dimensional Living Words, you begin to hold a tone that is recognizable in those higher dimensions. Your tone is aligned with *who you came here to be*. *She looks so present and happy; he is always so certain and gracious.* It is at this level that you not only start to become aware of being aware, you also become a conscious citizen of the fifth dimension.

Over these coming months and years, events will occur in your world that will hone and refine you, making you more specific, precise, clear and masterful. You will be able to more easily and naturally vibrate in frequencies that demonstrate *who you came here to be*. To get there from where you may be right now requires focused attention on your intention, as well as practice wearing the Living Words until they are well anchored, effortless and simply *who you are*. The higher fourth dimensional platform contains words or vibrations, which, if you begin to play with them, will make this transition quite smooth and enjoyable. By holding your attention on I AM Certain, I AM Capable etc., your physical and emotional bodies match that energy and outwardly demonstrate this to the external world. Far more importantly, however, those higher vibrations are presented to the Universe where the Law of Attraction acts to give back to you exactly what you hold your attention upon.

A triangular platform upon which to stand

This transition and Shift have nothing to do with anyone else. It's all about you and how you choose to vibrate.

- Find your space, become quiet and focused. Review the tools in Section II if necessary.
- Be in *present time*, and feel the sensation of being Powerful as in Capable. Simply allow the feeling of two Living Words, Powerful and Capable, to fill you up. There's nothing to do, no place to go. There is nothing to fix, because nothing is broken.
- Once you're feeling Powerful with Capable, change one word. Try Powerful with Graciousness now. Notice the difference in how you feel when you substitute this new word.
- Explore a sense of Graciousness. Relax and be curious. Allow and enjoy the changed energy. Notice how it feels different than Powerful and Capable. Powerful has no sword; there is no force or push. It is as if you are the very caring parent giving guidance to a small child.
- Once you have a solid experience of the energy and feeling of those two words, add the word Commanding—Powerful, Gracious and Commanding. You are creating a solid triangular platform upon which to stand.
- Notice how this combination of three Living Words feels in your space.

If you can weave all three of these words and energies together and wear them as an overcoat or stand upon them as a stable platform, you'll find that it's all about you in the most glorious of ways.

If it is difficult for you to hold these particular words, try combinations of three words that are more familiar and easier to reach. Begin simply. Orderly, Appreciative, Calm. Amused, Quiet, and Precise, for instance. The best word of all is Happy.

"I AM Happy." In our workshops, when we suggest the word Happy, many participants say, "I don't know what Happy is." In actuality, they have at some point in their lives experienced being Happy, they have simply forgotten, or let it get pushed aside by the life others have suggested they lead. Once they remember that moment and that feeling, the smile becomes grand on their faces. They are rediscovering, rewiring, realigning and remembering themselves.

As you begin to play with combining three Living Words, owning and internalizing them, a number of very specific things will begin to happen:

- **Your colors change.** Every word has a vibration of sound and color, and when you go Home each night you are recognized and known by your colors. You are a hue-man being: *hue* as in color, *man* as in form, and *being* as in spirit. As you begin to wear these words and own them, your colors change.

- **The words and their vibrations begin to be anchored in your energy field.** The words and their vibrations begin to be a demonstration of *who you are*. In addition to changing how others see you, the words also change how you respond and move in relationship to others. Consciously wearing these higher vibrational words begins to neutralize the vibrational tones that you have created unconsciously, out of habit. Like the Rose, these words vibrate at a higher, faster level. They are aligned with the highest energy that you are—an energy that quiets, smooths and releases all things unlike itself.

When you radiate the energy of the higher dimensional words, any words that are lesser, fall away. Ugly vibrations such as victim, lack, fear and *I am not okay* can no longer maintain themselves in your presence.

- **You begin to activate aspects of your Light Body.**
  Within the memory banks of your Soul, there is a blueprint, or schematic, of your Light Body. This is the body of Light, which you own and experience simultaneously in the higher dimensions. This is the vehicle that you use to move between the universes and through all of consciousness.

Every time you wear and *be* one of the higher dimensional words, a receptor within the Light Body reactivates. As the receptor turns back on, that word becomes fully anchored in your life. From that moment forward, you automatically demonstrate yourself as this energy, . As your Light Body begins to be more and more reactivated, your physicality becomes less dense—Light-*er*. You remember more of *who you are* as a higher dimensional being. Your Light Body demonstrates a harmonic resonance with the Creator and you demonstrate more fully the unique spark of the Creator that you are, but have forgotten.

Below is a short list of wonderful words and traits that you may want to incorporate into the foundation of your Light Body. Begin with one word, fully *be* it, then add a second. Then choose a third and think of these as a triangular platform upon which to build this new foundation. Feel them as you become them. Are there some in this list that you are unfamiliar with?

Adventurous	**Motivation**
Determination	**Neutrality**
Delight	**Optimistic**
Responsiveness	**Tender**
Accomplished	**Creative**
Dynamic	**Purposeful**
Kindness	**Telepathy**
Elegance	**Courage**
Aligned	**Clarity**
Spontaneous	**Cooperation**
Abundant	**Patience**
Attentive	**Honesty**
Erudition	**Compassion**
Lambency	**Communicative**
Artistic	**Integrity**
Leadership	**Insightful**
Enthusiasm	**Punctual**
Balance	**Wisdom**
Flexible	**Respectful**
Steadfastness	**Radiance**

MORE ON THE POWER OF WORDS TO REWIRE

Scan the QR code below or type the URL into your browser to access a page that contains a meditation to enhance your understanding of the Living Words

*www.masteringalchemy.com/
mabook-ch26-powerofwordstorewire*

CHAPTER TWENTY SEVEN

The Benefits of Mastering Your Attention Point

Perhaps you can now begin to see and understand the extreme value of mastering your attention point and how doing so is one of the things that will help you step out of the third dimension and into the high dimensional way of life. The following are some notes that will fill out this understanding.

Shifting your attention point without *going to*

Going to is the action of moving your attention out, away from yourself in order to observe something. Your friend says, "Oh, look at that interesting shape over there." And instead of staying on your internal observation deck, you leave the Center of Your Head, move through multiple layers of 3D noise and mentally *go to* the shape. As you leave your point of observation to experience that shape over there, you are no longer balanced and aligned within your field. You have wandered away from yourself. *Going to* causes a wobble in your perception and in your experience of the thing you are observing. What you see is distorted because you are not viewing it from your balanced, internal point of observation. What you might observe from the Center of Your Head as a red circle becomes a green square when you move through all the third dimensional noise and drama to see the shape. What makes *going to* additionally disruptive is that when you finally return to your internal observation deck, you must again pass through those multiple layers of the third dimensional noise, thoughts and emotions. Returning to the Center of Your Head or Higher Mind requires focused attention to disengage from what you *went to* (that shape over there). In other words, when you return your attention to the original point of observation, your awareness has been distorted by the noise between you and what you *went to*.

When you remain in, and observe life from, the Center of Your Head or Higher Mind, you more clearly see what you are observing without getting engaged or affected by the noise and emotion of *going to*. Viewing life from your observation deck, and not *going to* what is outside of you, allows you greater balance, ease and *choice*, You are not moving back and forth, or working to untangle your attention point and regain your balance. Understanding this concept and learning not to *go to* is one of the most important concepts you will ever learn. Mastering this skill is required for living in the fifth dimension.

Observing without labeling

Another aspect of mastering your attention point includes observing without labeling. When you begin to observe the world around you without labeling it, you begin to quiet even more of the noise that prevents you from knowing yourself. You break the habit of thinking, analyzing, identifying, rattling off information, and talking in your head. That habit is a lower layer of thought, and it is very noisy.

This is where many unnecessary questions come from. Questions like: *Why did he do that? How did that thing get there?* Or

What does she mean by that? In that lower layer of thought, you cannot find yourself among all the noise, most of which has nothing to do with you anyway.

Learning to observe without labeling requires intentional practice. To begin to disrupt this habit, first notice when you are observing and labeling. While watching three men move a box, are you commenting in your head as to why? Are you wanting to tell them a better way to lift? Are you thinking about what might be in the box; what the box reminds you of? None of this has anything to do with you and is simply more noise. When labeling something you observe, your thought process creates an electrical charge, which in turn keeps your internal noise actively engaged, thereby preventing you from experiencing higher levels of awareness.

Using the conscious, continuous breath as a tool for focusing your attention point

When you breathe in a continuous fashion, without stopping at either the inhale or exhale, you take another huge step in mastering your attention point. You also begin to take greater steps in remembering *who you are*, putting yourself back together, and building the bridge back to the Mother-Father-Creator. As you breathe in a continuous, uninterrupted, circular loop, the air begins to move into and out of your lungs in a deeper and fuller manner. The Pranic energy, which is the connection to the infinite intelligence of the Creator, can then be activated within, around, and through you at your command. Intentional creation is also expedited with this intelligence within the breath. It is this uninterrupted breath that activates and opens your ability to remain in fourth dimensional *present time*. It helps you remain focused upon your intention and your *now* experience, instead of drifting between third dimensional past and future. When we stop breathing at either the inhale or exhale, our awareness is also interrupted and sidetracked. Observe the next time your breathing halts. Where were you at that moment? Most likely, you were not in *present time*, but instead, were engulfed by a thought that was in the past or the future.

What you will notice as you become more masterful

As you begin to master your attention point, you quiet the noise and still the motion within yourself and within your life. There are many benefits to this:

- You begin to allow new, expanded choices to present themselves.
- You are more curious to see what a situation holds and less inclined to assume you know what is possible.
- As you begin to see subtleties and opportunities in situations, new possibilities open up.
- You find yourself less and less in the third dimensional experience of reacting to circumstances and more and more in the higher dimensional experience of *choice*.
- You begin to better sense your own truth and discern it from the truth of others.
- You begin to integrate the knowledge and wisdom of the Higher Self into your consciousness.
- You find yourself consciously choosing to be silent and not in motion.
- You notice the greater degree of noise in the lives of others without the need to engage.

- You find more amusement and curiosity in all you experience.

Scan the QR code or use the URL below to access an audio file in which Jim describes how to master the continuous breath.

www.masteringalchemy.com/mabook-ch27-continuousbreath

CHAPTER TWENTY EIGHT

Tricking Your Brain Into Awareness

If you have practiced meditation, you are familiar with a meditative state of awareness. In this place, you are very still and quiet, highly aware, observant, and in *present time*. Your mind is calm and open; your body relaxed and in a state of ease. You might feel expanded and leave your body with a feeling of floating. The meditative state is also known for producing increased creativity, enhanced learning, reduced stress and awakened spiritual abilities, such as clairvoyance. However, this wonderful state of awareness isn't just for meditation. It is possible to maintain this state of quiet observation while moving about your daily life. All of the tools and information we are sharing with you here lead to this ability; the ability to experience your walking around life from a higher state of conscious awareness.

There are many states of awareness, but for the sake of simplicity, let's say there are only two:

1. Eyes open, walking around through your day—engaged with others, thinking, planning, working, and doing.
2. Eyes closed as you rest or meditate—highly aware, observant, stress-free and in *present time*.

Something important occurs as you move between these two states of consciousness. Every time you close your eyes to rest, sleep, or meditate, your brain wave pattern changes. It flips between these two very different states of reality or consciousness. The movement between these two states is not questioned because it has been occurring since the first time you blinked. It has become one of our many unconscious habits and patterns. Like other unconscious habits, it is also possible to release this one.

One of your goals on this journey is to increase your ability to maintain a conscious focus and choose your experience, rather than being scattered and inattentive to what is before you. By practicing the tool of being in the Center of Your Head, and looking out from behind your closed eyes, you are drawn into *present time*. From this *present time* moment, it is possible to interrupt the flipping from one brain state to another. You can begin to maintain a consistency in your conscious awareness and attention, become much less affected by the third dimensional noise, and anchor your presence in the fourth and fifth dimensional consciousness—with your eyes open.

As you began to meditate, years or months ago, most likely you developed a well-worn path to get into that good-feeling place. It is also very likely that you continue to follow that path or routine even to this day. You light the candle, sit down in your usual chair, adjust your body, close your eyes, take a few deep breaths and begin your meditation (or begin to battle with the chatter in your head). When your session is over, you open your eyes and continue with your day. Three things are occurring here:

1. A very strong habit or routine has been created.
2. When you close your eyes, your brain flips from one state of brain activity to another.

3. When you open your eyes, your brain flips back, automatically.

You move from the meditative state back to the state of 'the real world'. Our goal is to disrupt that pattern so you are able to maintain that state of enhanced creativity, learning, and awareness throughout your day, not just during meditation. To disrupt this pattern we must take a two-pronged approach. We must address both the routine you got yourself into, as well as the flipping or changing of your brain pattern.

Changing the routine

The purpose of changing your meditation routine is to become more conscious of the pathway you have created and make it deliberate instead of by default.

- First, notice what you are doing now to prepare for meditation. To make the process conscious and real, write down the steps you take to prepare and go into meditation.
- Over your next few meditations, begin to mix up and change your routine. Don't change everything simultaneously. Doing so might not be necessary and might prevent an easy transition. For instance, instead of sitting in the same chair in the same room, break the pattern. Sit in a different chair in the kitchen instead of the bedroom. Or sit in a different corner of the room than you usually do.
- After you have lived with one change for a while, it will become familiar. When it does, move to another

option. Instead of using your gong, use a bell. Instead of the years-old prayer, create another. This is very much like strength training at the gym. When the body repeats the same routine too frequently, it plateaus and no long benefits from the workout. A new routine is necessary.

Creating a new pathway—an exercise

What do you do after you close your eyes? Do you take the same path each time? Our goal is to disrupt the habit of the brain flipping from one state of awareness to another automatically, without your management of it.

- Find your space, Grounding, Higher Mind, Octahedron, etc.
- Be very aware of your breathing and keep it going in a continuous loop without pausing or stopping at the inhale or exhale.
- Keep your eyes open and locate an object or spot on the wall in front of you at about eye level or slightly above. Choosing a point below eye level can create the tendency for your eyes to close.
- Look at that spot and hold it in your awareness as you take a breath and simultaneously allow your eyelids to close while you continue to see the spot through your closed eyelids. Don't *remember* the spot. See it.
- Breathe again and simultaneously open your eyes with your awareness on the spot.
- Breathe your eyes closed again and see the spot.
- Continue to repeat this for eight or ten breaths. On the

final breath, leave your eyes closed while continuing to look at the spot. You will notice you have more clarity than after your usual meditations.
- You may now continue with any other energy tools you would like to play with during this session.

The purpose of this exercise is to create an alert, focused, *present time* awareness that allows you to choose the direction you wish to experience, rather than drift somewhere away from yourself or go unconscious. If you find you are losing your focus, or your posture has shifted during your session, breathe your eyes open again, focus on the spot, and then breathe your eyes closed again. Repeat until the level of your clarity has increased again. This exercise creates increased clarity and consciousness in your meditations. You will remain sufficiently alert to practice your tools, yet you can still reach the expanded space of awareness without leaving your body.

When you incorporate this exercise into the non-meditation, walking around part of your day, you will also notice results. Taking a moment occasionally during the day to practice breathing your eyes open and closed while remaining conscious and focused on a spot, will bring you back to that alert, clear, meditative state of awareness. Practice before a meeting or important phone call. Practicing before and during a creative endeavor will allow you greater focus of attention on the project and, therefore, greater satisfaction and success. Soon, it will become a way of life.

As you begin to hold the same awareness, whether your eyes are open or closed, you begin to dissolve the veils of ignorance and forgetfulness that deflect much of your awareness of the higher dimensions. The brain no longer flips between two different levels of perception and awareness. As you practice this in combination with the other exercises in this book, your walking around life will be more like the focused, quiet alertness you can access in your meditations.

The QR code and URL below will take you to a page containing two audio files containing exercises specifically designed to help you trick your brain.

www.masteringalchemy.com/mabook-ch28-trickingbrain

CHAPTER TWENTY NINE

Understanding the Difference Between Your Higher Self and Your Soul

In almost every lecture we offer, someone will ask: "What's the difference between my Higher Self and my Soul?"

This is a great question and one that all of us have asked in one fashion or another. In our spiritual journey, we each are exposed to many terms; some easily understood, others confusing, and still others that are seemingly contradictory.

In simple terms, your Higher Self is a part of your Soul. It is the highest aspect of *who you are* that can be attained, anchored and held within the physical body. Your Higher Self is the part of you that knows, sees, and understands at the highest possible level available to you while you are in human form. Anchoring the wisdom of the Higher Self into your physicality is very much a part of our human spiritual evolution and purpose.

Your Soul, through the Higher Self, had an enormous role in choosing and designing what you experience in this lifetime. Your Soul wanted to become masterful and experience itself in a variety of different circumstances and experiences. So it put in place a plan and a process where it could do this—YOU.

Here's a simple example: Let's say your Soul wanted to know what it would be like to experience the feelings of embarrassment in a female body. So it placed part of its own consciousness in you, as a female body, and you then went out into this third dimension to experience the game plan that your Soul wished to have. You were born into a family of graceful dancers, yet you were clumsy and awkward and often fell down. You surrounded yourself with very simple, third dimensional children and you had a creative mind but no filter, so you blurted out things that later made you squirm and get funny looks from others. As an adult you liked to party, and many mornings found yourself uncomfortably explaining your actions of the night before.

In the process of these wonderful experiences your Soul created for you, you also have free will, which, in addition to what your Soul's desires were, allows you to choose and create many other components of this life-game. You choose to take dance lessons, and you learn to think before you speak, and to pace yourself at parties. You become more masterful and soon the embarrassing situations no longer happen so frequently. Your Soul is satisfied with this one experience. Of course, your Soul has many other experiences it wants to experience through you in this lifetime. You've mastered embarrassment and now you get to become masterful at tidiness, for example.

This amazing time of Shift is adding to how you experience both your Higher Self and your Soul. As you begin to remember yourself and return to higher levels of consciousness, aspects of you and your Higher Self will merge very rapidly. As you begin to experience yourself as the merged Higher Self, you begin to become more discerning, observing choices before acting. You will also begin to notice you have access to greater levels of knowledge, wisdom, understanding, and choices. This is you, the Higher Self and Soul becoming One in awareness.

Simultaneously, your Soul plays an enormous role in All That Is. Your Soul plays much more in the non-physical realm of consciousness, which is much vaster than the physical realm. To put it into perspective, imagine the concept and the reality of physicality as a single grain of sand on a beach. Everything else (everything) in All That Is is non-physical. However, most of us humans only know what we know, so physicality is *all* we know. In actuality, we are much bigger than our physicalness, but most of us don't know that yet. We only know what we know, and we don't know what we don't know. As you complete the agreements you made with your Soul (i.e. experiencing and mastering embarrassment and tidiness), the veils between you and your Soul become thinner and transparent. Soon, you and your Soul re-merge into one, and *who you are* becomes conscious, vast, and beyond third dimensional limitations.

As you intentionally awaken and merge with your Higher Self and your Soul during this Shift, you are doing something that has never been done before. As you intentionally focus upon your personal evolution, you will become much more aware of how your Soul plays and demonstrates itself in the physical. And it is through this awareness that you will also begin to build a bridge back to the Heart of the Creator.

CHAPTER THIRTY

The Higher Purpose of Your Ego

There is an aspect of you in the third dimensional reality known as the 'ego'. Many of us have been taught to believe the ego is a problem and, therefore, something we want to eliminate. Many on their spiritual journey do battle with the ego and see it as the nemesis of their spiritual growth. The ego has been blamed for getting us into social trouble and causing us to say and do things that are not in our highest good. As you move about your day you can recognize when others act from, and are motivated by, this unconscious demon. The spiritual goal of many traditions involves the dissolving of the ego and once that occurs, one's own true, Higher Self will be experienced and demonstrated in the world. Let's take a moment and view this aspect of us from a different platform.

Consider that the ego is an important, valuable part of your spiritual experience in a physical body, rather than something to kill off. After all, you have it in your life for some reason. As you begin to vibrate at higher levels of energy, you will find that your ego is actually a part of your Soul's blueprint, your Soul's plan. You intentionally included this in your third dimensional experience for a very important and valuable purpose. Instead of being an enemy to fight with, the ego can instead be viewed as another tool on your tool bench. Its purpose is to test you; to give you little challenges along your path so you may better refine your abilities and perspectives in order to grow and evolve yourself. The ego's job is to help you step up to higher and finer platforms and to help you become *who you came here to be*.

If you want to become a master gardener, you would learn how to grow your vegetables in complex weather conditions and in the microclimates of your area. You would be continually challenged to understand how much water, sun, and nutrients your tomatoes need, and how that mix is different from what your cucumbers need. You would also want to learn how to prevent insects, deer, and rabbits from devouring your crops. If you're going to be a master of this fifth dimensional reality, you will also be continually tested and given new circumstances to navigate, much like the conditions that challenge the gardener. It is as if the ego is saying, "You did a great job with that situation. You kept your mouth shut and didn't respond. Now, under this new, yet similar circumstance, what will you do? And with this other situation before you, how do you choose to respond? If part of your life's challenge is to master courage, then, in this situation," the ego says, "how do you choose to demonstrate courage?"

As you continue to move forward and step into the higher fourth and fifth dimensions, the ego stops being as active or dominant as it was in the third dimension. You have passed most of the challenges now. Henceforth, you will respond to the ego's challenges from a broader, quieter platform of awareness and with less reaction.

So if the root of all suffering isn't the ego, what is it that gets in our way and plants those nasty opinions and thoughts into our heads? What is it that makes us do and say things that we may later recognize as not what we really meant? These sloppy, self-destructive thoughts don't just occur overnight. You didn't just suddenly find yourself feeling defensive, taken advantage of, or fearing confrontation. You were not suddenly unfulfilled at work or in life. What happened was that single, individual thoughts repeated over many years, compounded to become beliefs, habits and then unconscious behavior patterns. The ego's job is to help you identify those so that you may release them.

As you begin to live and play upon a higher platform of awareness, you will begin to see opportunities to step out of this game. But this is really not about getting out of the third dimension, for that will happen soon anyway. It's about *mastering* the third dimension. It's about understanding how to play with the vibrations of the higher dimensions while you are in this body. The ego is a wonderful tool to help you master duality without being affected by it. You will soon be able step into simultaneous time and choose the possibility that you wish to experience. It's all available, but it's a very different consideration than the ones we've had available to us up to now.

CHAPTER THIRTY ONE

Your New Life In the Fifth Dimension

When you integrate the tools and information offered here into your daily life, and they become a part of *who you are*, you will no longer be affected by the third dimensional density and drama. You will be living your life on the higher dimensional platforms of community, grace, wholeness, co-creation, well-being, and much, much more.

So what awaits you in the fifth dimension? Before we describe that, let's first briefly review the structures of the third and fourth dimensions.

Third dimension = rigid structures

The third dimension is conditional and structured in a rigid density. It is heavy and operates with a specific set of rules and has certain characteristics, aspects, boundaries, edges, mutations and structures. It is very stable with limited flexibility. You rely on the rational, analytic mind, versus your ability to observe, perceive and choose, which are fourth dimensional characteristics. There are three main structures sustaining the third dimension:

- **DUALITY**—A dual mode of perception: the contrast between good/bad, right/wrong, positive/negative, should/shouldn't, up/down, black/white, cause and effect.

LINEAR TIME—The perception that time only moves in a straight line (one direction) and is experienced as past, present and future. The only *present time* in the third dimension is *reactionary present time*.

RATIONAL MIND—The GPS of the third dimension. The analytical, reasoning, thought processor designed to make comparisons, draw conclusions, store information, calculate, and make determinations. Its job is to keep you safe and have you fit in to the third dimension.

Fourth dimension = flexible structures

Much less structure and rigidity exist in the fourth dimension; it is open, receptive, and allows all possibilities. It is a dimension of choice and observation, and it operates as a more flexible platform without the rigidity of the third dimensional box. The fourth dimension provides us with an opportunity to reframe our reference points, review our beliefs, and attain a new understanding of what is possible. It allows us to be *in* the third dimensional world but not *of* it.

To recap, in the fourth dimension you have:

PRESENT TIME—This is your point of power. Each *now moment* is a threshold to new beginnings and fresh choices.

CHOICE—The power to choose consciously to initiate a different choice in any moment, as opposed to reacting to what shows up.

PARADOX—Flexibility. Something that was true a moment ago may not be true in the next *now moment*. By observing from *present time,* you have the increased awareness necessary to make a different choice in every *now moment*.

ALIGNMENT AND BALANCE—A state of equilibrium, which allows for opposing forces without reaction to what is before you.

So here in the fourth dimension you have *present time*, *flexibility* and *choice* to create as you wish with balance and alignment. If you can recognize and play with those three building blocks—*present time*, *flexibility* and *choice*—they alone will create an entirely different universe for you. You will find you open back up what you closed down when you came onto the third dimensional platform. You will re-engage your intuition and spiritual abilities and re-access your internal guidance system and your connection to the Creator.

The fourth dimensional platform begins to be the life you live, and third dimensional reference points such as, "Ain't it awful?" and "Why did they hurt my feelings?" simply dissolve. You may already be noticing that you are beginning to lose those reference points, along with all the other third dimensional aspects that aren't about *who you are.* Those old habits of thought and emotion are still available to be chosen, however, from this fourth dimensional point of reference you will choose them less and less often.

You are the creator of your game and it's only about you. No one else. It's *all* about you. How masterfully have you spent these last many lifetimes, training for *this* particular lifetime? You are training yourself to remain standing on this fourth dimensional platform when your limitations, habits, and 'stuff' come up and threaten to shove you off. And we can say with great certainty that your stuff *will* come up—relationship stuff, job stuff, money stuff. All of it. But from this different fourth dimensional *present time* platform you will begin to choose differently.

Your stuff—*everyone's* stuff—is now being amplified by the Shift. It will be very helpful to anchor yourself firmly on that fourth dimensional platform and allow the *who you are not* to gently leave. On this fourth dimensional platform you can choose to let it go much more easily. If you grab hold of your limitations and habits, argue with and try to figure them out, or if you turn away and deny them, you have jumped right back to the third dimensional platform. You can choose to look at it and release it now, or later, but it will return louder and stronger if you choose not to own it, and use your tools to release it. At some point you will stop arguing for your limitations, take a breath, smile, and say, "Maybe I *can* just let it go." By allowing this to occur from that fourth dimensional platform, the arguments become much softer and the limitations become less important.

This fourth dimensional platform is a stepping stone to the fifth dimension, which offers you a life beyond your imagination. Life in the fifth dimension operates mostly outside the grasp of the rational mind. The rational mind cannot understand or fit fifth dimensional experiences into its box. The rational mind will fabricate stories about what the fifth dimension is but does not have the capacity to experience it. It is only from the fourth dimensional platform that you begin to access and experience a fifth dimensional awareness.

The door to the fifth dimension

Although most of us have touched this quiet, expansive place, there are very few words that adequately describe life in the fifth dimension. The fifth dimension offers multiple possibilities that exist in words like *joy, happiness, stillness, enthusiasm, community, cooperation, respect, appreciation* and *creation*.

The density of the third dimensional structure is too heavy, rigid and resistant to be held in the light, airy fifth dimension. Simply put, you cannot take your limitations and baggage with you. It is impossible to enter the fifth dimension while holding a third dimensional vibration. It isn't that you are not allowed, or are kicked out, or forbidden access to the fifth dimension. It is similar to a hot air balloon trying to reach a higher elevation while carrying too much weight; your third dimensional vibration is simply not a match to the energy vibration.

It is very possible, however, to be a citizen of the fifth dimension walking in a third dimensional world, creating from the platform of the fourth dimension. And you will be stunned and joyful at the ease with which multiple possibilities move and flow happily in this higher, faster, clearer co-creation process. It is creating in excitement with others, and allowing multiple possibilities: "Together let's make this happen, and then we can do this. We could add three of these, two of those and what about this?" It is from this fifth dimensional experience that you play and create with new tools such as the Rays of Creation, the Triads, the fifth Element of Love, and the Christed Matrix. It is from a fifth dimensional consciousness that you experience the Holy Spirit and the aspect of the Creator known as the El Shaddai. All the elements and applications are at your fingertips, and they joyfully come together allowing you to create effortlessly with a single thought and a joyful feeling in your heart.

Alchemy happens when you live in the fifth dimension. The mastering of Alchemy is found in curiosity, inquisitiveness and application: learning to utilize sound, color, and geometry to weave, shape and form. Magnetism, electromagnetism, patterns of Light, feelings of Beauty and higher aspects of Love all come together to form the complexities of universes as well as the simplicity of a drop of water on a morning lily. Alchemy *is* the very fabric of creation in the fifth dimension.

Time in the fifth dimension

Time also exists in the fifth dimension but in a very different configuration than previously experienced. Once fourth dimensional *present time* is understood and experienced, time shifts into Simultaneous Time. Simultaneous Time allows you to see the broader perspective of All That Is. It is here where all things exist in the same place at the same moment. In the fifth dimension there are no past or future lives, no parallel or alternate lives. All that you have ever been and ever will be is accessible in this dimension of consciousness at the same moment. All the answers to your questions lie exactly where each question is asked, and you are able to broadly view all possibilities before choosing an action.

If you can begin to live the qualities and possibilities of the fourth dimension, entry to the fifth becomes available to you very quickly. It is far beyond the rational mind even to begin to grasp the qualities, aspects and life in the fifth dimension. The fifth dimension vibrates at a very high, brilliant and fast frequency range. Heavy, dense thoughts and emotionally charged vibrations such as reaction, anger, judgment, and fear cannot be held in the fifth dimensional realm. In the fifth dimension there are no limitations. All possibilities are available for creation in Simultaneous Time.

Standing on the platform of the higher dimensions

The group of Archangels and Ascended Masters that we have the honor to create with has asked that these tools and information be offered at this time because the opportunity to move into higher dimensions is now real. It will become very visible to you in the coming months and years. So rather than being surprised and reactionary with the choice of fear, or "How come no one told me?" as amazing events unfold before you, you can prepare by firmly positioning yourself on the fourth dimensional platform. Be happy—you're *really* going to enjoy the results.

This opportunity to stand on the higher dimensional platforms without falling back into the third dimension is very available and immensely important. Look at all the institutions, structures, games, economics; all of man's inhumanity to planet Earth and her inhabitants, and know that it will soon be brought into balance. Standing on the higher platforms will keep you out of fear, and help you experience this unfolding with fascination. Imagine if someone invented a little box that had the capacity to draw electricity freely out of the atmosphere. Suddenly, every house in the world could be electrified, heated, cooled and have plumbing and hot water out of this little box. Do you think that would shift the whole balance of the game? Absolutely. It is stunning to watch this dance unfold, and it doesn't even have to be dramatic.

On the other hand, the majority of humanity is not awake and will remain in that third dimensional fear. As you, however, begin to master the higher levels of being, you will walk through the seams of time, drama and noise, unaffected and radiating the example of what is possible. Choose to stay in the third dimension, and the noise will get very loud. Our passion is for this higher awareness to begin to flow in your space, so you can simply nudge the person next to you and say, "You know, you *could* stand on that train track as the train is rushing toward you, or you could just step over to this platform with me and let the train go right on by."

The long-awaited 'Shift of the Ages' is upon us

You chose to leave the wonderful Home of the Creator and dive into the third dimension. When the Creator wanted to know Himself/Herself better, She/He asked for volunteers, and guess who ran to the front of the line, pushing others out of the way shouting "Pick me, pick me. Send me!" YOU!

The Creator smiled and said, "Let me explain this third dimension. First it is very dense. It is dark. When you arrive you are going to forget *who you are*, and you are going to forget who I AM."

"Wow!" You said. "Sounds interesting."

"You will experience a great variety of contrasts. You will try on many costumes and experience many choices. To do all this, you are going to put a big bag over your head and wander around in this darkness until you find you way back Home."

You and many others got very excited about this new adventure. Something new in All That Is does not happen often.

You said, in great excitement, "About this darkness thing… How deep can we go?"

The Creator, very pleased, smiled and said, "As deep as you would like. Turn over all the rocks and stones. Open all the doors. Explore, ask, wander and discover, so I can 'Know Myself'.

And you said, "Watch this!" as with great enthusiasm and laughter you jumped high and dived deeper into the darkness so you and the Creator could know more.

The Creator sent the brightest and the best (you) on this special quest to explore the outermost regions of existence. It was and is, a grand adventure that only the biggest and most enthusiastic spirits signed up for. We have taken this third dimensional adventure as far as we can. We explored this diverse, dense duality and have been wildly successful at what we set out to accomplish. A huge vibrational upshift (on every level) is what the Earth and her inhabitants are undergoing right now. You are a very important part of this Shift. You are big, not small. You are significant, not insignificant. You make a difference, and your contribution is valued by all of humanity, and by All That Is.

This is a Grand Adventure, an adventure that was never thought to be possible. What and how we are creating together is being observed from every corner of all the universes. There is amazement, admiration and great joy in the hearts of the observers, as they watch the grand finale unfold. We are not only unraveling ourselves from the third dimension; we are creating a new Home—a new Heaven on Earth in the higher dimensions.

And as spectacular as this is, there is more…

Unveiling the experiment

There is an opportunity before us that was never previously thought to be possible for these times. In co-creation with the Archangels and Great Beings of Light, there is an opportunity to bring a new pathway forth; one that is created through the hearts of the most passionate of humanity; those who have returned to hold the dream of bringing Heaven to Earth. This pathway is an experiment, a grand experiment.

As the third dimension is being dissolved, ALL of humanity will move forward on a path to return Home, leaving the third dimensional density behind. Some will take one path; others who are the most unconscious will take a different path, but *all* will return Home. Here's what will happen:

Those who are less conscious, or slower to wake up, will take a slower path that does not lead straight to the higher dimensions, but rather, takes them to a place where they will have the opportunity to learn everything that those who are already conscious and are making the Shift have been experiencing. Once they have learned what you have learned and are able to *experience* it for themselves, they too will be ready to enter the fifth dimension.

Because you are reading this book, you have an opportunity to make a different choice. The Archangels saw an opportunity to provide a set of tools, and a series of choices and experiences, which, if followed, will enable you to bypass the incremental steps that mass consciousness will experience on their path, and thus greatly accelerate your journey Home.

Revealing the *true* nature of the experiment

Our passion and purpose is threefold: first, to introduce you to this new pathway, second, to provide you with some of the tools that will enable you to make this journey and transition, smoothly, comfortably, and elegantly, and third, to reveal to you *the true nature of this grand experiment…*

YOU are the experiment.

YOU are being asked to awaken and walk this accelerated pathway with the desire that, as you once again become the fully conscious *Being of bright Light that you are*, others will see your Light and follow you back to the Heart of the Creator.

It was hoped in the year 1987 that a small group of humans could align a vibration of Light so brilliant that a crystallized doorway of evolution could be created. By the time we entered 2012, that glimmer of intention had become a radiant flame of Light, which is now being firmly held by those who have been brave and determined; those who are remembering and beginning to understand that not only are each of us *not* little, as we have erroneously thought, but we are BIGGER, MORE IMPORTANT and MORE SIGNIFICANT than we have ever imagined.

And, most importantly, YOU count. You are the Light that appears at the top of the candlestick for all in the house to see. And as you awaken, realign, rewire, recreate and remember yourself, *your* vibration is beginning to awaken the rest of the world.

Today, the experiment is unfolding, and you are stepping up to be the healer, teacher, leader you came here to be.

Be pleased with yourself.

It is time for you, for all of us together, to go Home, to return to the Heart of the Creator.

*You are no longer the body
negotiating this Earthly experience.*

*You are the creator… creating, directing,
in a very precise way.*

*You are only using the body so that
your creations can be manifested into
the world of matter.*

*And you have opened a pathway for
others to follow… to come into that
unified consciousness with you and create
and express through their individuality,
through their perfection, as do you!*

—METATRON, AUGUST, 2012

Success Stories

The following are segments taken from letters we have received from students over the past few years. We offer these, not as 'boasts', but rather as a testament to what can be achieved with the tools of Mastering Alchemy, many of which are presented in this book, as well as in the free articles and webinars that are available on our website and YouTube channel, which you can subscribe to at *www.youtube.com/masteringalchemy*.

Free Webinars
"Tonight's class was phenomenal for me. Both your lecture and the Q & A period were extremely helpful. There was a huge shift—a lot of releasing of very old, unproductive patterns. Thank you so much for holding that space and for your clear explanations. See you in Arizona at our conference."

—*G.M., HOLLAND*

"I think the webinars and the DVD are masterpieces and I use your teachings every day in my life. I am 55-years-old and have been on a search for love, peace and harmony all my life and you're helping me achieve it with the mastering of Alchemy. I look forward to Level 2."

—*C.H., BRAZIL*

How the Tools are Changing My Life
"Your book *Spirit Matter*s played a significant role when I had to deal with a second diagnosis and treatment of breast cancer. My medical team got me through the physical healing, but using energy tools from your book helped me discard stress and anger. I now greet each day with confidence and smiles. I am well again."

—*J.S., LATVIA*

The Octahedron
"Last evening we had just begun to eat in a restaurant when ear piercing shrieks from some child erupted every few seconds. The third time I put my hand over my ears and cringed. Then I remembered my Octahedron. I distorted the right side to send it way out into the restaurant. The shrieks stopped immediately. I didn't see the child or its family, so don't know whether it was just a coincidence, but it worked! We both enjoyed the rest of our meal in peace and harmony!"

—*B.H., CALIFORNIA*

The Rose Tool
"My husband returned from work with a painful, swollen foot. So he asked me for a healing. I used the Rose tool and saw it expand and explode and dissolve. I could see and feel the swelling go and his foot became normal. The pain left and he slept well all night. I love you and thank you from my heart for sharing these techniques with us."

—*P.R., NORTH DAKOTA*

"The first four days of chemo were difficult. I just wanted to be still and rest. By the time I was getting my fourth chemo, while looking at the bag of liquids, I had a feeling of anger and repugnance. I realized I had to work all other areas of my being and start accepting the chemo bag. I also used the Rose to dissolve all side effects and got into my Octahedron. I rested profoundly until the fifth day when I woke up feeling great, no nausea, able to eat, talk, read, and be happy. Thanks again for your Love and time."

—A.S., TENNESSEE

The Living Words

"I've watched Level 1 three times and every time I get new insights. I use these very simple tools now every day. Every morning before I get dressed, I dress myself with these Living Words and it works so wonderfully. It is a beautiful start to my morning meditation. My mind is much more quiet."

—C.E., VIRGINIA

Setting the Energy

"Yesterday I had an amazing Rose experience. Usually our business meetings are depressing and on top of it the engineer giving it is like Mr. Data from Star Trek: devoid of emotion and emotional reactions. Fifteen minutes before the meeting I set about using the Rose at the center of the room. I filled it with fun, amusement, laughter, cooperation, harmony and good communication. The results were nothing short of 'miraculous.' The engineer directing the meeting was at ease. He laughed and smiled a lot and stopped and listened to every single question. The people in the breakout groups worked with such fluid harmony, the engineer was surprised at the results. Overall, a fun and productive meeting. Thanks so much."

—W.S., MEXICO

Grounding Cord
"As a spiritual healer, I am not unfamiliar with the Grounding Cord, but this is the clearest and most effective explanation of it I have come across and I love it! The concept of sending 'useless' stuff down the Grounding Cord is new to me and having it set up is so easy, in daily life as well as in my work. I am already feeling more calm, stable and capable, and most importantly, I am no longer feeling 'lost in the woods' about what lies ahead. Another huge thing: I no longer feel alone or isolated on my path."

—K.M., NETHERLANDS

Pink Diamond in the Sacred Heart
"I have completed the Level1 'Creating thePersonalPower Field' DVD set. The journey into the Pink Sacred Heart, connecting with the three Kingdoms, and the story of Atlantis were so powerful for me. The first time I took the journey, tears streamed down my face as I connected with the animals, elementals and angels that I had so long forgotten. I listen to this journey often and I feel my dear loving friends drawing ever near to me."

—W.C., NEW MEXICO

"The Level 1 course is amazing. Like pieces of a puzzle, each session helps connect/bring the fragments together. Although I have to say, the Pink Diamond session moved me to tears of Joy. There are no words to express the feelings of Love and Grace, Power and Compassion, Joy and Wisdom. With very little effort I can feel myself standing in the middle of my pink diamond along with my Soul, my Higher Mind and my dodecahedron. This is me… this is who I AM. This is where I choose to live."

—J.H., IRELAND

Money and Career
"How to manifest tuition: I took your Level 1 Course. A few days after ordering it I was laid off from my job along with most of my department. So when I completed your workshop and saw that there was a six-month course for the outrageous sum of $995, I rolled my eyes and muttered, 'Yeah, right.' I was concerned about paying rent and eating.

But after the course, which I bought because the Rose Tool has proved to be one of the most valuable things I've ever experienced (I've roto-rootered out so much stuff—and it doesn't come back!), I decided to put your tools to the test. I got my Octahedron spinning and… I threw it out there to the universe: 'Send me $995 for Jim's class.' But nothing happened… Until that afternoon, when I got a call from a company that hired me on the spot. No interview, just based on my reputation, they brought me in with a 30 percent pay raise. I began the day after I did my $995 meditation.

Friday, I got my first check. It was pro-rated since I started at the end of a pay cycle. The check was for $995. Exactly! Your check will go out tomorrow and I can't wait to join you for Level 2."

—D.T., COMPUTER PROGRAMMER, OREGON

Level 1 Program
"Mastering Alchemy is both practical and profound. What I have learned has allowed me to transform chronic issues and to create realities that I didn't think were possible."

—S.B., RETIRED BANK EXECUTIVE, GEORGIA

"Many thanks for the magnificent lessons that you bring! For the first time in thirty years I can relax and sleep without being awakened by panic attacks."

—D.H., EGYPT

"I look forward to each session very much. So much is happening, so very fast. I can feel the veil physically lifting every day, and as it lifts, the vision of Heaven on Earth becomes less of a dream and more of a reality. It is exciting to be here at this time. I am so grateful for your commitment to this."

—J.V., CFO, FLORIDA

"Wowie zowie, is what I have to say about how this work changes family dynamics. I am on such a different level with my kids. There is nothing missing and much to be gained by staying in that 4-5D space."

"I visited my kids for Mother's Day and have never had such high level conversations or participated in a family project before. Most times my son-in-law finds very little to talk with me about, and almost never generates the conversation. But this time, we were all completely present, full of love for each other and involved the whole four days. We even created a 40" x 60" painting of their trip to Paris. It was non-stop conversation and excitement."

—S.S., IRELAND

The Level 2 Program
"The Level 2 program has given me the tools and freedom to acknowledge 'who I am.' I now have an understanding of what my purpose and Soul's agreements are."

—L.R., EXECUTIVE ASSISTANT, WASHINGTON

"In session #1 you stated that the rational mind cannot conceive where we are going. You were right on. I've known we all are in for a wonderful experience, but last night was incredibly wonderful and there is no way I could have guessed what we would cover or experience. During the session, when I met AA Gabriel, tears began to flow—tears of joy. The experience of meeting AA Metatron was, well, he just took over me and enveloped me. We all are in for a real treat of experiences during the coming months. Thank you SO much for making these experiences available."

—J.P., GEORGIA

"I had thoracic surgery several months ago and I use many of your meditations and I must say I feel happier every day. I went in for a CAT scan last week. The tumor on the lung is reduced by 50 percent. I know that this energy is moving through me; I am entering full recovery. I have no words to describe the impact of all the tools and teachings you are sharing with us. My appreciation, gratitude and love are always there for you and your angels, Masters, etc."

—*E.B., MINNEAPOLIS*

"For many years I have been working on the restoration of hearing in my right ear. As the surgeon who had operated on me 35 years ago severed the nerve by mistake, nothing was possible medically. That hasn't stopped me from trying to do it for myself using the MA tools.

In the last week or so, I have been aware of strange movements within this ear. I tried listening to Jim (Lesson 45) with my earphone against my right ear and there he was! Not just muffled sound, as I had always imagined my first re-introduction into the world of sound from that ear would be. I cannot even begin to describe my joy when I heard that familiar and much-loved voice through the right ear. Perfectly clear and no need to turn the volume up. I didn't need proof that MA could lead us into miracles, but I am sooooo very grateful to be able to hear again."

—*J.E., AUSTRALIA*

"On Sunday morning I noticed a growth on my dog's eyebrow that appeared suddenly and seemed to get larger throughout the day. Not a big enough problem to go to the pet hospital (very expensive), but enough of a problem for a call to the vet Monday morning. Sunday night I listened to the Level 2 Lesson 23 (Introduction of the eighth Ray) class. Monday afternoon I went to my mother's house and mentioned the growth and she said (as she, and I, and others have said a million times) 'It's always something, isn't it?' And of course, we always mean it's something bad or inconvenient.

I was thinking about that on my way home and realized how many of those phrases are still in my consciousness— 'life's hard and then you die; nothing's sure in life but death and taxes', and so forth. What a wonderful job for the eighth Ray!

I fully expected my dog would need some type of surgery to remove the growth. Throughout the day I was thinking that it would be nice (fourth layer of thought) if surgery could be accomplished without general anesthesia. No fear or trying, just 'wouldn't it be nice…' So Monday evening, I used the eighth Ray to remove the phrase 'It's always something,' and all related strings. Tuesday I went to the vet. The assistant looked at my dog and said, 'Yep, it's a growth,' then went and got the vet. The vet looked at my dog.
VET: 'Yep, it's a growth… but she's young to have such a growth. Hmm. Wait a minute, this looks like a tick.'
ME: 'A tick?! I didn't know we had ticks in Alaska.'
VET: 'Yes, but they're very rare. Has your dog been

running in any overhanging brush?'
ME: 'Yes, of course. He's a dog.'

So the vet pulls out some huge tweezers, and carefully removes the tick. We chat for a moment, then I go out to pay for the visit. The receptionist says, 'Oh there's no charge for this visit. See you next time.'

Thank you for the Rays of Creation, Jim."

—D.S., ALASKA

"This morning I woke up feeling pretty negative; long string of heavy thoughts, feelings of complete overwhelm, and fatigue and irritation. For just a few moments I found myself enjoying the bitchiness… then I took a breath, stepped into the fifth dimension, smiled, and moved it all into the second Ray of Creation in the pineal. The feeling was breathtaking and miraculous, and for the first 20 minutes of my morning walk I just kept shoveling it all into the light in the pineal and into the star tetrahedron in the heart—the overwhelm, the 'why me,' the 'what's next,' and the aches and the pains. I must admit, I laughed out loud and I didn't care what anyone thought. Thank you."

—C.K., NEW ZEALAND

The Level 3 Program
"I grew up in communism and a patriarchal culture (Romania) where women were, by default, 'lesser'. I was also yelled at a lot, which challenged me to 'be better'. So I 'better-ed' myself my whole life and I was/am very pleased with the results. Yet there were still things

I wanted to 'do' for this 'better-ness'... like finish my paintings, get a successful exhibition, publish my books, etc. When I walked into Mastering Alchemy at 10-10-10, I was shown a whole new level of 'better' and soon enough in Level 2 I wanted to 'be' like Jim & Roxane. It was just so awesome to finally have mentors.

When I finished Level 2, I was so happy with all the 'better-ness' I'd accomplished, I even considered taking a break from MA. Today, three-quarters through Level 3, I find myself so Happy and so Pleased with Myself that I don't want to be like Jim & Roxane anymore, I want to be like Me, because I'm pretty awesome and quite beautiful just as I am. (I-wanna-be-like-Me!) Now this is a whole new level of being Pleased with Myself, isn't it?"

—C.S., ILLINOIS

"On Thursday, after re-listening to Level 3 Session 54, I tripped and fell headlong onto a cement floor. I could feel the effect on my shoulder and my knee and especially my wrist, which I had used to stop my fall. I lay there for a second or two, beginning to think about what could be hurt, then immediately cut off the thought and said out loud, 'I AM OK.' I stood up and walked away as if it hadn't happened. There wasn't even any stiffness the next morning!

Red Ray and Yellow Ray, Will and Power, Love and Wisdom! I am so thankful for these Mastering Alchemy tools and am deeply honored to be part of our World Service Project."

—M.B., CANADA

"As I was driving in to Chicago today, I got this ache-y, burning pain in my shoulder. I thought 'where did this come from?' Right away, I called upon the eighth Ray and said if this pain is someone else's please remove and return their energy to them. I then called upon the El Shaddai to remove any residual energy that might be remaining. Shin Dalet Yod. Instantaneously the pain stopped, it is four hours later and no pain."

—R.S., ILLINOIS

Epilogue:
How Do We Know All This?

People often ask how I know what I know and how I come by the information, tools, and techniques that I teach. The answer may surprise you.

Ever since I was a child I have enjoyed full recall of what happens to me when I am asleep. Each night when I go to sleep I pass through the astral realm and experience myself very consciously in the higher etheric realms, which is a most wonderful place. In these realms I get to play consciously with the Angels, the Archangels and all the Great Spiritual Beings of Light. Right now, the excitement about this 'Shift of Consciousness' that is currently taking place on Earth is the focal point of almost everything that is happening in the higher realms.

Each morning when I wake, I awaken with full and complete memory of what happened during the night, including where I went and with whom I played. I feel extremely blessed to be able to sit at the table with these great beings of Light and to experience this amazing orchestration of events. More importantly, however, I would also like you to know that every night YOU too sit at the same table; not as a visitor, but as an equal; for this is where you also go during those eight hours of sleep that you do not remember.

Let me also make it just as clear that whether you are just waking up and discovering this new adventure, or whether you have been playing the Game of 'bringing Heaven to Earth' for some period of time, contrary to what you have been taught to believe, YOU are very significant. You have always been very significant, and it is now time to remember *who you are*.

It is time to realign yourself, to rewire yourself, and to recreate yourself, so that you too can once again remember and re-experience all that you have forgotten you know.

It is time to remember your purpose, and to assist all the others behind you—those who are just waking up as well as those who have yet to wake up—to remember their purpose.

It has been specifically requested by the Archangels and Great Beings of Light that these tools to remembering *who you are* should be presented and made available to all who wish to participate in this experiment.

Since I have been asked to assist in this process, it is my desire, my passion and my privilege to provide as much information as possible; hence you will find many lectures, articles, tools and skills, along with audio and video clips presented freely for your growth and understanding on our website.

For those who are ready to go even further, all of the tools, skills and concepts outlined in this book are taught as part of the Level 1 'Creating Your Personal Power Field' Class, which is available as both a DVD set, as well as an online streaming program.

For more detailed information about our Free Membership and Level 1, 2 and 3 programs, see the final section 'What is Mastering Alchemy?' at the back of this book.

ABOUT THE AUTHORS

Jim Self

JIM SELF is an international teacher, speaker, author (*Spirit Matters: Down-to-Earth Tools for a Spirited Life*), and leader in the field of spiritual development.

One of the few teachers, authors and speakers actually working at the leading edge, providing solid, up-to-date information and practical energy tools to help us keep pace with the Shift, Jim walks with a foot in both worlds.

At the age of twenty-six, Jim was elected to his first of two terms to the San Jose, CA City Council and later became the Vice Mayor. Before completing his second term, he was asked by President Jimmy Carter to be an advisor and the Director of Governmental Operations for the Dept. of Energy. As an entrepreneur, he has successfully built and sold two corporations, and is the founder and current Board Chairman of a third biomedical corporation.

At the same time, Jim has had the ability since childhood to recall his experiences within the sleep state. Over the last twenty years, this awareness has expanded into relationships with the archangels, ascended masters and teachers of Light. The tools and information presented in the program, Mastering Alchemy, is a co-creation of these relationships.

Jim has been leading seminars on personal energy management and the tools of Mastering Alchemy for over thirty years.

Roxane Burnett

ROXANE BURNETT was a successful art director and manager for two major corporations for many years prior to taking the leap of faith and starting her own design firm. At night, she taught the tools presented in this book and was soon faced with the decision to jump off another cliff—to teach and coach full time. She has never looked back.

Presenting this work live throughout North America, Roxane is also the co-author of *Spirit Matters* and has been offering tools for developing intuition and personal power to individuals, businesses and professional women's groups since 1994. She has been featured on television, radio, and in national publications both in the US and Australia.

Roxane is the co-founder of Mastering Alchemy, manages the business, website, and the many volunteers. She joyfully creates and presents this work with Jim.

WHAT DO YOU MEAN THE THIRD DIMENSION IS GOING AWAY?

What is Mastering Alchemy?

Alchemy is much more than the concept of changing lead into gold. Alchemy is a way of life, a pathway allowing you to step from your third dimensional experience into a higher, more expansive awareness of life.

In order to experience the mastering of Alchemy and accelerate your ascension as a multidimensional being in this human form, the Archangels and the great Beings of Light have constructed a tangible pathway. This pathway is comprised of a number of steps, which together form the Mastering Alchemy Program.

The Mastering Alchemy program is designed in five segments. The purpose is to provide you with as much information as possible to assist you in understanding the third and fourth dimensional rules and structures, and allow you to recognize that much of who you believe you are, actually has very little to do with *who you are*.

Step One - Free Membership for Understanding the Shift

On our website there is a significant library of free information in the form of essential energy tools, previous webinars, lectures, articles, radio and TV interviews. In addition to these resources, special live lectures and webinars focusing on important changes occurring within the Shift are provided throughout the year for those on the mailing list. These special live events also include question and answer sessions to better help you understand this current 'Shift in Consciousness', and how it is affecting you and the world around you.

Step Two - Level 1

This is where the Mastering Alchemy Program starts to get really exciting. The purpose of Level 1 is to rebuild your Personal Power energy field. This is accomplished with a specific set of sacred geometrical tools and applications, some of which have been shared with you in this book. Understanding how energy is organized, moves and is directed is fundamental to your growth. By rebuilding this energy containment field and aligning the core geometry of the Octahedron, you create an antenna, which enables you to access the frequency of your higher dimensional consciousness and your Higher Mind.

Ascension requires you to enter the Sanctuary of the Pink Diamond within the heart, reunite with your Soul, and remember what your Soul knows. Here you will access the Still Point and enter into Oneness with the Mother/Father Creator.

How Will Your Life Change?

Level 1 can help you:
- Quiet the noise and drama in your life
- Master the art of remaining unaffected by the increasing chaos of the world
- Leverage the power of the Seven Living Words
- Dissolve the self-limiting habits and patterns that were imprinted upon you as a child, but were never yours
- Access the Inner Sanctuary within your Sacred Heart, create a conscious, intentional connection with your

Soul, and know all that your Soul knows
- Unify the masculine and feminine aspects of yourself
- Balance your brain's hemispheres
- Remember who you are and what you came here to accomplish
- Discover your role as a Healer, Teacher and Leader
- Begin to see with your eyes closed
- Learn how to ease ascension symptoms
- Change your DNA coding, increase your oxygen levels, and anchor your fourth and fifth dimensional chakra systems
- Learn to use the Rays of Creation
- Hear and feel the Language of Light spoken
- Remember your role in Atlantis.

Level 1 is a pre-requisite for Level 2

Step three - Level 2

Level 2 has been specifically designed by the Archangels for those who wish to accelerate their ascension and is the core work of Mastering Alchemy. Its purpose is to:

- Clear the density from your mental body by neutralizing disempowering thought habits and patterns
- Clear the magnetically charged emotional patterns and conditioning from your emotional body
- Activate the internal Living Light Body, transforming the cellular density of your physical body into liquid golden Light. This is the pathway of ascension.

In order to accomplish this, we must shift from thinking with our rational mind to thinking with our Heart and acting from the intelligence of our Higher Mind. This occurs by integrating the true meaning and experience of such words and concepts as Certainty, Capable, Happy, Graciousness, Commanding and Focused as platforms upon which to live your life. Living from these specifically crafted platforms allows you to observe and move within the world around you without engaging with the noise and drama of the third dimension.

From this expanded point of observation you will begin to utilize your inherent skills of clairvoyance, knowingness, and your natural ability to communicate with your higher consciousness and the higher dimensional intelligence. Many precise tools, applications, and experiences are provided in this work to assist you in anchoring these connections and integrating all these skills and information.

What will you experience?

- Continue to fully merge with your Soul and to know what your Soul knows
- Meet Rose of Light and the Orange Dragonfly
- Transform early childhood conditioning held within your DNA's memory Discover that the answers to your questions are found exactly where the questions are asked
- Rewrite your past and re-craft your future
- Transform the Octahedron into the Star Tetrahedron
- Visit the Temples of Purification and Resurrection within the fifth dimension
- Dissolve the veils of forgetfulness and ignorance
- Activate your hypothalamus, pineal and pituitary glands

- Create and experience your Well-Being Platform
- Realign the fourth chakra, thymus gland and the fifth chakra
- Understand and use the fourth, fifth, sixth and eighth Rays of Creation
- Anchor and activate the Cube as your personal environment for creations
- Work and play with your new chakra system—the Triads.

New Level 2 groups form every three months in November, February, May and August.

Step four - Level 3

A short time ago the Archangels explained that the next level of work is to bring the Ascension process itself forth. This ascension format has never been experienced. It is an experiment and YOU are the experiment.

The Level 3 program is a co-creation between the Archangels, Ascended Masters and you, a physical human. In order to reach their goal, they have asked to co-create in each session, actively teaching and providing verbal instruction. Level 3 is an ongoing program in yearly segments. It is un-ending.

Here is some of what we play with in Level 3:
- Clear the density of third dimensional thoughts and emotions to such a level that these two bodies will become one.
- You will merge this mental-emotional body into the spiritual body, becoming one with the Soul. This is done consciously within the fifth and sixth dimensions.

From this level of Soul consciousness, the lower three chakras are reconfigured, balanced, and raised to a new vibrational level.
- This new alignment then gives you access to the Unified Field of Consciousness for the first time in your physical form. This access opens conscious awareness into the Universal Mind of the Creator and allows you to experience the Holy Spirit for the first time. (The Holy Spirit is not what we were trained to think it is.)

What will you experience?

- Alter the electrical function of your brain
- Activate the 90% of the brain that is turned off
- Alter the neurological and electromagnetic functions
- Change the hormonal production of the pituitary gland to fully regenerate the physical body into perfect health
- Integrate the Soul, the Over-Self, and Spirit into a singular living alignment in the Heart
- Fully access and become ONE with the 'Christed Over-Self'... and more.

If you would like to sign up for a Free Membership and gain access to our free articles, audios, videos, webinars and essential Mastering Alchemy tools, *visit www.masteringalchemy.com/become-a-member*

The QR code and URL on the next page will take you to a page featuring a video and links to MP3 audio files, in which Jim explains more about what Mastering Alchemy is and what is very possible for you.

WHAT IS MASTERING ALCHEMY?

www. masteringalchemy.com/what-is-mastering-alchemy

NOTES

NOTES